Shad Helmstetter, Ph.D.

The
Gift

To:

_____

From:

_____

The
Gift

ShadHelmstetter, Ph.D.

PARK AVENUE PRESS

Acknowledgments

This book is dedicated to the many consultants who personally gave so selflessly of their time for the research on this book, and to all of the Arbonne people everywhere, who are doing so much to change lives for the better.

S.H.

The Gift

Helmstetter, Shad
      The Gift

ISBN 0-9727821-4-1

Printed in USA

10 9 8 7 6 5 4 3 2

The Gift
By Shad Helmstetter, Ph.D.

Table of Contents

Foreword

By Rita Davenport

You're going to love this book, and you're *really* going to love what it will do for you.

I first met Shad Helmstetter years ago when I hosted a television show in Phoenix, where I interviewed him several times on my show. I remember thinking then, after listening to his approach to life, that this man could change the life of any person for the better who took the time to listen to his message.

Like many others, in the years between then and now, I embraced his personal growth message, and I have read and recommended his books to a great many people. But this one, *The Gift*, is the best of all of them. It brings the best personal growth tools all together in one book, and makes all of them easy to understand and easy to put into practice. It is practical, effective and powerful.

As you read *The Gift*, keep a highlighter nearby, or a pen to make personal notes. It's that kind of book. It is also a book to keep close by when you are facing some hurdle in your life, because one of the twelve tools offered in this book will surely be able to help you get back on track.

Shad Helmstetter shares my goal of helping as many people as possible during the time we are given to be here. I believe this book will go a long way toward doing that. (In fact, it truly is the book I would have liked to write myself.)

The Gift, and the twelve personal tools it teaches, will change lives. It offers clear reasons why some people struggle to move forward in many areas of their life—yet always seem to remain in the same spot (or move backwards). It describes simple steps to take to initiate lasting and permanent change—from changing "self-talk," to setting goals, to taking action now. Dr. Helmstetter goes beyond offering hope; he shines a light on a true and healthy path for people to follow to improve their lives.

This book is truly a gift that "keeps on giving." I am grateful to have received this book for its many benefits, and I look forward to sharing its powerful message with so many others. Shad Helmstetter has been a treasured gift in my life. I owe him much.

Rita Davenport
Scottsdale, Arizona

Chapter 1

The Gifts that Make Your Dreams Come True

Y ou have the most *amazing* life in front of you!
No matter where you've been, who you are, or what you've done with your life up to now, your life, from today on, is just *beginning*.

It doesn't really make any difference what you've done in your job or career, how much education you have, what problems you've had in the past, or how much money you have in the bank.

The only thing that counts is that you are *you*, right now, today—and you were born to live an incredible life. A life that is filled with promise and potential. You were born to be

3

the best of yourself, and to bring that "self" to life.

If you choose to live up to the promise you were born with, you have the chance to do that. You get to *dream*—and you get to make your dreams happen. You get to be the "you" that you were born to be in the first place.

What Stops Your Dreams From Coming True?

All of us, at one time or another, have dreamed of having a life that has magic in it. A life that's special, and filled with wonderful things. But in time, many of us stop dreaming. We learn to believe that dreams are one thing—but *life* is another. And when we look at our life each day, we sometimes don't see much magic in it. Because we don't have a way to make those dreams come true, we stop believing that we could ever live that wondrous life we dreamed about. So we stop believing in our dreams. Then we stop dreaming. And then we forget how.

Many of those dreams we dreamed were absolutely practical dreams, of course. They may have looked magical, and almost too wonderful to hope for, but they were entirely possible. If we could only have found a way to reach them, a way to make them happen!

But when we can't find a way to bring our own dreams to life, we start to believe that the idea of living a special life is reserved for *other* people—but not for *us*. We even believe that other people are more fortunate than we are, almost as though *they* were destined to live out their dreams, but we weren't.

When you see other people living their dreams, while your

own dreams seem to have become nothing more than vague memories or forgotten wishes, it's not "fortune" that separates your life from theirs. In all likelihood, you had as many opportunities in front of you as they did. And your natural, inborn potential was, and still is, just as great as theirs.

So how, then, are some people able to dream, keep the dream alive, and then make it come true—while so many others, *just as capable*, are *not*?

The answer isn't luck or fate. The answer isn't your potential. It isn't your education. It isn't your financial strength. And the answer isn't in your background, or what you've done in your life up to now.

The answer is in the "tools" you use to reach your dreams.

The People Who Reach Their Dreams
Have Learned to Use the Tools

There are twelve almost magical tools that were given as gifts to all of us. Some people learn to use each of these tools—but most people learn to use only a few of them. The people who reach their dreams have learned to use *all* of them.

I'm not referring here to the gifts of talent, or skills, or abilities that one person may have, and another person may not. The tools that make dreams come true were given equally to each of us—and they were given to you. All you have to do is know what they are, make them your own, and use each of them.

The people who use the tools succeed—that is, they make their dreams happen. People who do not use the tools, or use

5

only a few of them now and then, never really live their dreams. Instead, they watch the other people succeeding, and wish it could be them. They convince themselves that it's luck or fate, when it isn't that at all. It's the *tools*.

The Twelve Gifts

What are these gifts—these almost magical tools—which, when you use them, make your dreams come true? They are:

The Gift of *Surrounding Yourself With Success*

The Gift of *Choice*

The Gift of *Helping Other People Grow*

The Gift of *Believing in Yourself*

The Gift of *Changing Your Self-Talk*

The Gift of *Exceptional Attitude*

The Gift of *Finding Your Focus*

The Gift of *Setting Great Goals*

The Gift of *Taking Control of Your Time and Your Life*

The Gift of *Putting Yourself Into Action*

The Gift of *Never Giving Up*

The Gift of *Doing Something You Love*

Together, those twelve gifts make up the most important tools for personal growth I have found in over thirty years of research in the field of human behavior and motivational psychology. They are the best of the best. When you use them, your most incredible dreams begin to come to life.

That's not a fairytale notion at all. As you'll find, it is these tools that are at the source of all personal growth. They are the most *profound* and the most *practical* tools that achievers have ever used. In fact, these tools are so effective, so powerful, that when you use them, what happens next almost seems like *magic*.

Entire books have been written about each of these twelve tools, and I've had the privilege of writing several of them. But my purpose here is to present all of the essential tools together, as a *primer* and a reminder—and I've summarized each of these tools in a way that you can apply them immediately in your own life.

It's Time to Dream Again

More people would be willing to dream, if they knew they had a way to make their dreams come true. But as I said, without seeing a clear way to reach our dreams, we stop believing. Why keep dreaming, if there's no chance of the dream ever *happening*?

But if you *knew* you had all of the tools you needed to reach any good goal you set, wouldn't it be wonderful to dream again—and to know that your greatest dreams could come true?

For now, to get started, there are only two things you have to do. The first is to *trust*. You can trust that, if you use the tools, you *will* reach your goals. I've watched these same

7

remarkable gifts change the lives of *tens of thousands* of people. None of the tools is difficult to use, and when you use them, they will work just as effectively for you.

The second thing you have to do is to be willing to *dream* again—*really dream*. No matter what you may have dreamed of in the past, or where you are in your life right now, take the time to dream again—and be willing to imagine *anything* at all.

The greatest stories about people, and what they achieved in their lives, are the stories of those people who chose to *dream*, and then went on to make their dreams come to life. (Not surprisingly, there are *no* great stories written about people who have no dreams.)

If you're willing to *trust*, and if you're willing to *dream*, with these twelve gifts—the tools that make your dreams come true—one of those stories could be about you.

What Would You Like to Do Next?

Think for a moment about what you would like to do *next*. Or what you would like to do with the rest of your life. (That's something to think about.)

Whatever you're doing in your life right now, or whatever your own greatest dreams might be, I encourage you to use the tools you'll find in the following pages. As you read through each of the "gifts," think seriously about your own goals, and how you can apply these tools in your life now.

Whether you want to make your career work better, become more independent, follow a new direction, or find a more important part of yourself, the twelve gifts you'll find here will help. As I share with you the twelve tools of personal growth in the chapters that follow, and as you think about your own personal potential, I think you'll find that your future is alive and well—*and* you'll have help finding out what to do next.

Putting the Tools of Personal Growth Into Practice

During the years I first wrote about the tools of personal growth, I noticed that some people immediately put the tools into practice, while other people never really got into the habit of using them. They all recognized the value of the tools, yet some people used them, and others did not.

After observing many examples of these two types of people over time, the answer finally became clear to me. The people who rapidly began to use the tools, and continued to use them, in almost every case, were in a business or organization that trained, supported, motivated, and *encouraged* them to use the tools!

In other words, through their work activity, these people had a *vehicle* that helped them put the tools of personal growth into actual practice in their lives, both on the job and at home, day after day. The result was that they became dramatically more successful and fulfilled in many areas of their lives.

The second group, the ones who did *not* put the personal growth tools into practice, invariably had *no* real support network—no vehicle—that allowed them to apply the principles to their everyday life.

The Best "Support System" You Can Find

Over the years, I have seen the same picture repeated again and again. It is because of that awareness that I have so often recommended that if you want to improve your life, you should make sure you have the best support system you can find.

I also studied and researched companies and organizations to learn which of them fostered personal growth in their employees or members, and which of them did not. I was looking for the *best* of the best organizations—the ones that used the tools, and created a "culture of personal growth" in their membership.

I found some exemplary organizations, and by way of example, in this book I'll introduce you to one of my very favorites. It is an organization that has based its company philosophy and character almost *entirely* on individual personal growth, and it teaches and practices all *twelve* of the tools of personal growth that I'm sharing with you here.

In researching the best of the best, the company I've chosen is a positive role model of an organization that helps people get better. It's an organization that has given each of its associates and members an exceptional gift—the gift of lifelong personal growth.

I call it "The Gift of Arbonne."

Chapter 2

The *Gift* of Arbonne

F or many years, I've studied many different businesses and organizations, looking for those which offered people a *life*—instead of a *job*.

In that time, I've found a few exemplary business organizations that create a completely *positive* kind of work environment. The kind of environment that actually *builds* its members' lives by helping them grow—and becomes a "*support system*" for its employees or members.

Finding the Ones Who Are
Getting it Right

I call these organizations *"life changers,"* because they actually make an important difference in people's lives. They give people a way to apply the principles of personal growth and put them into practice, both on the job and at home. And in doing that, they literally change those people's lives.

If you're familiar with my work over time, you know that now and then I choose to showcase a particular organization that's doing it *right*. As a professional researcher and spokesperson in the field of personal growth, I seek out and find those groups that can stand up to scrutiny as a positive example for the rest of the world to follow.

The Story of Arbonne

One of the life-changing organizations that has impressed me greatly, came to my attention because of a long-time friend of mine, a woman named Rita Davenport. Rita herself has been an incredible life-changer for thousands of men and women.

I first met Rita many years ago during the time she was hosting a popular television show in Phoenix, Arizona, and she invited me to be a guest on her show. She was also a very popular motivational speaker who captivated audiences throughout the United States with her quick intelligent wit and down-home wisdom. She, too, had dedicated her life to helping people grow, and she was doing a good job of it.

Some time later, after we had worked together on one of

her early television projects, Rita went on to build a huge following—and a reputation that would place her at the summit of the world of personal growth. Her heart, warmth, and spirit made her the kind of leader who inspires not only respect, but also affection in all those fortunate enough to have their lives touched by her.

It would be some years later that our paths would cross again, and I was not surprised to see how far Rita had taken her life-building work. On this occasion, I was asked to speak for a highly respected skin-care organization named Arbonne International, which has trained thousands of positive-minded skin-care consultants throughout the United States. And at the helm of this life-changer organization, as the company's president, was my friend, Rita Davenport.

My First Close-Up Look at Arbonne

I'm often asked to speak to organizations, but I had never before spoken to an Arbonne audience. I agreed to speak to the Arbonne group, and since it would give me the opportunity to catch up with Rita again, I was looking forward to it. But even knowing that it was Rita who was the president of the company, I had no idea of the positive surprise I was in for when I flew into Phoenix to speak in front of several hundred Arbonne skin-care consultants.

The Room With a Glow

I first noticed it when I walked into the large hotel ballroom before my talk. And when I went to the podium a few minutes later, it was unmistakable. There was a *glow* in the room! I wasn't imagining it; it was there!

Throughout my entire talk, I noticed it, like a soft glowing light, radiating from the faces of the several hundred women, and a few men, seated in front of me. I remember thinking that it must be because all of them were skin-care consultants who were using their own products—and the glowing complexions must be the result. In that, I was correct. But there was something *else* I noticed—something that *added* to the glow.

The *Other* Light—The Light Behind the Eyes

What I also saw was an *inner* light—the light behind the eyes. The kind of light that's born of the most positive of attitudes, a spirit that's *alive*, and a sense of wellness. It was an uplifting experience. I was there to share my message on personal growth and motivation with them, and yet, here *they* were, inspiring *me*.

It was more than enough to make me want to find out more about these people with their remarkable glow, and the company that had brought them together.

Who Are These People—and How Are They Doing All These Positive Things?

What I learned about the Arbonne organization, even in my earliest research, is that their business philosophy is based

14

on the concept of *personal growth*—and helping *other* people get better. That concept, which I subscribe to so strongly myself, has obviously been working for them.

Here was an organization, made up mostly of women, who were building careers and futures based on motives that went far beyond financial rewards. The more I met and got to know people in their organization, the more I became convinced that they had created a business model—and in fact, a *lifestyle*—that was literally changing its members' lives.

I should have expected that in advance. Having known Rita Davenport, and the kinds of principles she had always associated herself with, I would have bet that any group she was a part of, would be not only a winning, goal-oriented organization—but also one that was filled with *heart*.

A Business Built on *Heart*

Over time, as I furthered my research into the Arbonne organization, I spoke to and interviewed many of its members—from every background and walk of life, and from every part of the country. But even though they came from broadly diverse backgrounds, their stories were uncannily similar. Each of them had, in one way or another, been introduced to Arbonne—and the gift it has given to so many women—and its *heart*. And because of that *one* chance introduction to Arbonne, each of their lives had changed—incredibly so, and for the better!

The more I interviewed them, and the more of their personal stories I heard, the more I could see why there are now *several hundred thousand* Arbonne consultants in the

15

United States. (And that number is growing rapidly.)

Fortunately, the unique "culture of Arbonne" is being carefully protected by Arbonne Chairman and CEO, Robert Henry. I've had the privilege of spending many hours in Bob's company as he shared his ongoing vision for Arbonne and its organization of consultants. I also found him to be a person of character—the kind of character and values that build people, and quality enterprises. (It's not at all surprising that Robert Henry is a highly respected leader in the network marketing industry.)

This is a man who cares about *people*—and all of the people in his organization especially. His strong background (in law, accounting, and business leadership at the executive level), his belief in the principles of helping people grow, and his absolute determination to maintain the highest standards of quality, mean that the gift of Arbonne will continue to be in good hands for years to come.

Putting the Tools Into *Practice*

What interested me about this company was that it was accomplishing all of the important steps that make an organization one of the life-changers. And even though all of the Arbonne "members" themselves are independent business owners, through a remarkable ongoing program of training and support, Arbonne had created a life-long program of personal growth for its independent consultants.

As a result, Arbonne has become a *vehicle* through which people learn and practice every one of the important tools of personal growth that I'm discussing in this book: the gifts of *sharing; making good choices; surrounding yourself with success; helping other people get better; learning to believe in yourself; learning new Self-Talk and getting a new picture of yourself; doing something that you love; finding your focus and staying on track; taking control of your time and your day; taking action; and never giving up.*

It was exactly those gifts—the tools of personal growth and the key steps to creating a fulfilling career and a successful life—that the Arbonne company had applied to the business of healthy skin-care and personal nutrition.

They were helping people get better on the *outside*—with unusually effective skin-care and nutritional products—and at the same time, helping people get better on the *inside*, with a deep-seated devotion to personal growth and individual achievement. In doing that, they became *life-changers* in the most positive and effective way.

A *Vehicle* That Helps People Get Better

With that kind of business philosophy, it was not a surprise to me that they were so successful. True quality always stands out. The people of Arbonne have taken a company with great products and great potential, and turned it into something exceptional. And in the process, they have created the kind of value-based, life-changing organization I look for. They meet the requirements of being the "vehicle" that can help almost anyone get *better*.

The closer I looked, the more I saw Arbonne as a vehicle for *growth* for all of its members—both financially and in their personal lives.

17

It was not difficult to recognize the Arbonne organization as a clear example of a way to put the tools of personal growth into practice. They were already doing precisely that, in thousands of individual lives, every day.

A Place to *Start*, a Place to *Grow*, and a Place to *Soar*

During the years that I've written a number of books in this field, I've found only a few companies or organizations that actually practiced all *twelve* of the tools of personal growth that I'm presenting to you here.

Arbonne teaches and practices all of them. It is a place of mind where people grow, and often soar beyond their dreams. There are other businesses and career paths that may offer similar life opportunities—but after hearing the personal stories of a great many Arbonne consultants, I found their positive message truly unique, and impossible to ignore. During the course of my research, I interviewed many people whose lives have been virtually *transformed* because of the Arbonne "gift."

It became clear to me that Arbonne is one of the exceptional, people-based organizations who have figured it out—they understand the difference between a "job" and a "life." They give people a place to *start,* a place to *grow,* and a place to *soar*.

Putting It to The Test

From my first look at the life-changing concepts that are espoused by Arbonne consultants, starting with that day I first spoke to a few hundred of them from stage, and saw the "glow," I suspected that the products they were offering must be pretty good.

Part of the glow I saw in that room, you will recall, was the result of something very healthy they were doing for their skin. As I began to meet more of the consultants, in conversations and interviews, I could not help but notice that, without exception, each of them looked youthful and vital, younger than their years. I don't believe in magical formulas, but I do believe in science and chemistry.

The Best Was Yet to Come

After my first talk to the Arbonne group in Phoenix, Rita sent me a kit of her company's "age-reducing" skin lotions as a gift for my wife. I appreciated the gift, and gave it to my wife but, for the moment, didn't think anything more about it. I was, by then, busy looking into the promising, "life-changing" personal growth benefits of Arbonne's business philosophy, but I had not yet focused my research on the benefits of the products their consultants were sharing with others.

Then, one evening, my wife walked into my studio where I was writing, and I looked up, and said, "What have you done? You look ten years younger!" And she did. Her complexion was more youthful, noticeable, and incredible. She had the glow. She had used the gift.

A few weeks later, over dinner at a favorite beachside restaurant, a friend of ours was seated across the table from us. I was delighted when our friend said almost the same words to my wife that I had said. "I can't get over your complexion," she said. "You look ten years younger."

During dinner that evening, our friend repeated her assertion several times, saying, "I can't get over it. You look younger. What are you doing to do that?" (Show any woman, and most men, a "fountain of youth," and you'll get their attention.)

I knew by then *why* my wife's complexion had become more youthful; I had seen the results for myself, and other people were noticing it, too.

During the same time, I had told Patricia Wright, one of my long-time friends, and a certified Executive Life Coach, about my research into the Arbonne business philosophy and the results my wife had experienced from using the products.

As it happened, one of Patricia's life coach clients was, herself, an Arbonne skin-care consultant, and she had sent samples of the same products to Patricia. Patricia was excited to relate her experience to me. After trying the samples for herself, Patricia's friends *also* began telling her how much *younger* she looked. I won't reveal Patricia's age, but it's over fifty. Her friends were telling her she looked *years* younger. (While Patricia remains one of the best life coaches I have ever known, she is also now an Arbonne consultant, and is sharing "the gift" with everyone she meets.)

Earning an Income by Helping
Other People Get Better

Not only has Arbonne helped people grow in many ways personally, but it has also helped people change their lives financially. I've met many Arbonne consultants who have gone from living with constant financial struggles—before Arbonne—to now having money in the bank and true financial freedom for the first time in their lives.

Many of the women I talked with were able to quit their workplace jobs, and earn more money than their old careers could ever have offered. Now they're earning more, but they're working from their homes. That's an idea I have always liked.

Often, people who became consultants and started sharing Arbonne with others, got interested only because they had tried the products themselves and were overjoyed with the results. It had nothing to do with money or financial rewards.

When they first got started, they modestly imagined earning a few hundred dollars a month in extra income. But then, almost as an unexpected "side benefit" of being a consultant, their finances dramatically changed.

"It's Not About the Income . . . But We
Just Bought a Beautiful Home."

In fact, a surprising number of new consultants, within some months of getting started, have found themselves leaving their old jobs—and their financial worries—behind.

As one mid-twenties consultant said to me, "It's not about the income . . . but we just bought a beautiful new home. We thought it would be years before we could do something like that."

Another Arbonne consultant, equally surprised by her success, had just received the keys to a brand new, white Mercedes, and she and her husband were about to leave on a trip to the Caribbean. "I got into this business because I wanted to help people feel better about themselves," she told me. "That's still why I want to be in this business. But we're going to have a great time in the Caribbean!"

I was happy to see that positive financial growth was a part of the Arbonne picture. I have seen over the years too many promising men and women who ended up losing their dreams—and doing nothing with their futures—simply because they couldn't afford to pay the rent.

So it's no wonder that I heard so many positive stories about Arbonne—and what it does for the people whose lives it touches. Someone has figured out how to help people look *younger*, get *better*, and get *financially free*—all at the *same time*.

There should be more businesses and organizations like that.

The Light That Never Fades

Since the first time I spoke to an Arbonne audience, I have spoken to many other Arbonne groups throughout the United States. But it doesn't matter where I go; if it's an audience of Arbonne consultants I'm speaking to, that same glow is always there.

As a writer and researcher, I have to remain outside and objective. But if I knew you as a close, personal friend, and if your own personal growth in life was important to you, I would suggest to you that you get to know Arbonne.

It's one of those very special organizations that actually change lives—for the better. It gives you a way to use all of the gifts of personal growth in your life—and they help you become healthier—*and look better*—at the same time. That's not a bad combination.

A Role Model for Others to Follow

I really like Arbonne. I like the company, I like what it stands for, and I especially like the people who are in it. It's a company with class. When I meet someone on an airplane and the subject of personal growth comes up, I'm always proud to talk about Arbonne and its people, like friends I admire and believe in. There are very few companies I would say that about.

In my field of personal growth, I look for those things that exemplify the best of our values and qualities. Arbonne is one of those that stand out. They're making a difference in the world.

Groups like Arbonne are rare. And it's very uplifting to me to see an organization in which thousands of individuals are "living" the best personal growth concepts and using the tools of personal growth, daily, in their own lives. (They also have one of the best on-going training programs of any of the organizations I have studied.)

I believe that organizations like Arbonne, and the independent business women and men who make up the organization, should be exemplified for what they're doing. It's great to see them growing, and they're having an incredibly positive effect on the lives of everyone they touch. So they're a great role model to follow. As I said, we could use more like them.

Using the Tools—and Having Help
Along the Way

When you use the tools of personal growth, you can do it on your own, or you can have *help*. People who have help reaching their goals almost always do better than people who try to excel on their own.

Since almost *all* of us want to look and feel our best, and since Arbonne helps people look and feel their best, while at the same time giving them a way to earn more income or become financially independent (both things I ascribe to), it makes sense to align yourself with other people who are already "doing it" and who will help you do the same.

You can, with enough work and self-determination, of course, reach your goals on your own. I believe in choice, and if that's what you choose to do, I encourage you to do that and win. Use the tools I've outlined for you here. Put them into practice on your own, one by one, and watch what happens.

But if you'd like to reach all of your dreams, and have some *help* along the way, experience has shown me that it's better to have a strong, positive support team that will help you get there. If you'd like to have an exceptional team on your side, talk to an Arbonne consultant and get on board—to whatever degree you want.

Whether it's the "business" part of the business or the personal growth part that appeals to you most, you'll get the help, the support, and the belief you need to excel. And you'll have a way to put the most important tools of living into practice, starting now.

Now let's begin with your first great gift—one of the tools that will give you immediate help in anything you do. It is the important gift of *Surrounding Yourself with Success.*

Chapter 3

The Gift of Surrounding Yourself With Success

T his is a gift that Arbonne has mastered—and teaches to every one of its members. If you're not already using this tool, I recommend you start now. It *will* make a difference!

To make it clear just how important this tool is, imagine that this gift is like a photograph. A portrait of you, surrounded by the people who will help you reach your goals and make your dreams come true. And the best part of the gift is that you get to *choose* who is in the photograph with you.

It's true that you *become* most what you *surround* yourself with most. So it should be apparent that you would naturally want to create the best "success environment" you can get.

But many people don't understand how important this personal growth tool of "surrounding yourself with success" can be. If you don't recognize the importance of this tool, you may give little or no thought to who or what takes up your *mind* space—the most important space you'll ever own.

You should, however, because what you feed into your brain can mean the critical difference between your success and your failure. With what we now know about how the brain gets programmed by the input we give it, you have an incredible opportunity to give it the *right* input.

You'll Only Go as Far as The People Who Take You There

Let's say, as an example, that you want to be, in every sense of the word, "successful." You want to *reach your goals, feel good about yourself, do something that is emotionally and personally fulfilling, have plenty of money in the bank, and share the good with others.*

Those are worthwhile goals, so to help you figure out how to reach them, we're going to take three photographs of you—three pictures of you, working at reaching your goals.

Photograph #1
In the first photograph, you're standing in a field. It's sort of a barren place, and you're in the middle of the field all alone. In this photograph, you can see from the look on your face that you're feeling kind of lonely. There's no one in the field with you; no one is there to help you reach your goals.

27

Photograph #2

The second picture of you shows you standing in another field. But in this picture, you're not alone. With you are dozens of people—the people who are in your life right now. Your family, close friends, people you work with, and even just acquaintances. In fact, this *is* the picture of you in your life right now.

So in this photograph you're no longer alone. You chose some of the people to be in this photograph with you, but most of them you didn't. They just showed up in your life—and they're in the photograph with you.

Photograph #3

In this picture you're standing in a beautiful meadow, and there are also other people with you. Some of them are the same people who were in the previous photograph with you, but there are also some *new* people who weren't there before.

When you look at the new faces, you immediately notice how positive they look, and that they look confident and intelligent, but also warm. And what's especially interesting is that the new people in your meadow are all people you respect, or look up to, or people you would like to be more like.

And *all* of the new people with you in the third photograph are people who *reach their goals; they* all *feel good about themselves; they* all *do things that are fulfilling; they* all *have plenty of money in the bank, and they* all *share the good with the people around them. Their* goals, and their ideals, are just like *yours*.

If You Wanted to Be Successful, Which Picture of You Would You Choose?

How did you do? How does your personal photograph look right now?

If you wanted to be successful, and you had to make a choice of which of the three photographs best predicts your most successful "life environment," which picture of you would you choose?

Photograph #1 is you, all by yourself. In that picture you're all alone. It's hard to surround yourself with success when you're standing all alone—so that picture of you would obviously not be a good choice.

Photograph #2 is you in your field, but you've only *personally* chosen a *few* of the people you really wanted to have in your photograph with you. The rest of the people in the picture just happened to be there . . . standing in the field of your life. Only a few of them have the same goals you do, or even think about goals all that much. It's hard to make a team when the right people aren't in the picture.

So, here again, if you want to be successful, this picture of you will *not* help you get there. It may have too many of the wrong people in it, and not enough of the *right* ones.

Photograph #3 is a very different kind of picture. It is you and your future success team—the people *you've* picked for yourself. The people you love are there, of course. But in this picture you've also included the people you admire most, and the people who can help you most—*and most of them are already successful.*

This is the photograph to have framed and placed where you see it every day. If other people's programs rub off on

29

you—and they *do*—*this* is the team that's going to help you get to where you want to go.

The People Who *Program* Your Success

Whoever is in your photograph with you will end up playing a major role in your success. That doesn't mean your success isn't up to you—it *is*—but the people in your photograph with you are the people whose own success "programs" will become *yours*. They are the influences that will *guide, motivate, support,* and *inspire* you.

These are the people who will be typing messages directly into your mental computer—the computer that directs your life. And they'll be giving you programs through everything they say and by everything they do. How they *think*, the *actions* they take, the kind of *character* each of them has, how much *confidence* they have, how much *spirit* they possess, and what their *values* are—everything about the people you choose to have around you will be giving your computer brain "input" that is vital to your success.

Your Computer Mind is Recording *Everything*

The quality of the people you surround yourself with is important, because your computer is *always* listening; it's taking the input even when you're not aware you're getting it. Critical to understanding this vital, unconscious aspect of the human brain, is that your own brain is taking everything in, and storing it as though it's necessary information, even when it isn't.

For example, when you spend time with someone who is very negative, you begin to notice that negativity rubbing off on you. Unfortunately, it's doing worse than that. Your brain is actually recording every word, every look, every nuance, and every emotion. And it's recording all that "stuff" as though it's important and worthwhile.

You get more of that same negative input every time you're around that person, so in time you have stored up megabytes of completely unnecessary, negative, counter-productive, destructive input *that your brain has stored—and thinks it's supposed to* act *on!*

That's why I tell people to avoid the dreaded Negatroids! And it's not just "try not to listen to them." If you're around them, your brain is still listening—and recording—even if you're trying *not* to listen.

Also Avoid the Idle Bystanders of Life— They Don't Belong in Your Picture

You may care a lot about people, but don't invite just *anyone* into your photograph. You can't afford to have the picture of your life filled with people who are just sitting this one out.

It isn't just the negative people that can hold you back. *Anyone* (or anything) that could hold you back should not be in your photograph with you! People who don't have vision, those who disbelieve, those who have poverty mentalities, people without goals or purpose, people who don't believe in your dreams . . . should not be in your picture with you.

31

That doesn't mean you should immediately avoid spending time with anyone who isn't a positive, active, motivated winner in life. But you do have to decide who you choose to spend most of your time with—and who you want to have in your photograph with you. And it's very important that *you* make that choice.

(There may, of course, be some people in our lives who are not supportive or positive-minded, but we're obligated for one reason or other to have them there. In that case, do your best to ignore or override the negatives, keep your own Self-Talk positive, and keep moving forward.)

Name the People You Want to Have *With* You in *Your* Photograph

If you want to be successful, this is an essential step—and it's something you can do, starting right now. Decide on the kind of people you want to have in the picture with you. And then, in real life, put them there.

I mentioned that Arbonne has mastered the gift of helping people surround themselves with success. It's one of the reasons they're successful. By their positive philosophy and people-oriented business style, they naturally create a group and a network of exactly the kind of positive, motivated people we're talking about.

Because "like attracts like," an organization like that naturally attracts other like-minded, successful, positive, go-for-it people, so that now, women and men who are a part of the organization are literally surrounded by the kind of people your parents probably wanted you to hang around with in the first place.

Because Arbonne attracts caring, like-minded people, when you're associated with that kind of organization, and you want to name the people you'd like to have in your photograph with you, you don't have far to go to find them.

Actually choosing and *naming* those people is an important step in using this gift. That process begins with recognizing that you *are* in a photograph right now. And all of the people who are populating your life right now are in your photograph with you. When you look at each of them, ask yourself *which* of them you would actually have *invited* to be in your picture. Which of them would you have *chosen*?

I'm not suggesting you immediately take most of your friends to the "Returns" window at the "friend store," and ask for your money back. But if you could choose now, who would you *most* like to have in your life, and whose "programs" would you like to have rub off on you?

Planning the Best Picture of Your Future

The great news in this gift is that you get to do something about the people who appear with you in your next photograph.

In a series of personal accounts called *"Eye On Arbonne,"* Arbonne publishes the stories of their advancing consultants, written by the consultants themselves. Along with their stories are the photographs that testify to their successes (and the *fun* they're having reaching their goals.)

In reading these personal stories, I've noticed that many of

33

the photographs include the people who helped those consul-tants become successful. In those photographs, you can see that in each case, the individuals who wanted to reach their goals have surrounded themselves with positive, like-minded people. They have literally *surrounded* themselves with success.

(To read these stories and see the pictures first-hand, you can go online to www.arbonne.com. There are many of these incredible stories there—and they clearly show why those people are successful.)

Take Another Photograph—and Add the People *You* Would *Choose* to Have Around You

Wherever you are in your life right now, stop for a mo-ment, and take a brand new mental photograph of the people who you would most like to have in your photograph with you. Not just at home, but the people you would most like to have around you in your *life*.

(This is also a gift that helps you have more *fun* in your life! Think of it—being surrounded by positive, upbeat, friendly people, doing things together that you really enjoy doing, helping each other succeed—and making friends for life.)

Who are the people, the influences, the coaches, the supporters, the believers and the motivators you would most like to have around you in your own personal photograph? Take a moment, or as long as you like, and think of the people who could help you most, who would be the most fun to have there with you. (Any ideas?)

Those are the people who, *if you place them there*, will give you the input, give you the best programs, share their successes and help you make your own dreams come true.

In the Picture of Your Life, *Everything* Counts

When you surround yourself with success, it is more than just the faces in the photograph that will count.

Who you surround yourself with is one thing. *What* you surround yourself with is just as important. If the world you choose to place around you is always typing messages into your life computer, it's up to you to control the *input*. What you're doing each day is actually setting up your success by what you surround yourself with most.

As an example, what does your home look like, and what messages does it give you? What pictures do you have on the walls? Do you have an office in your home, or do you use the kitchen table as your office? Have you created an environment that is positive, inviting, and makes you think and feel successful? Do you organize your environment so you'll have an organized mind?

What clothes do you choose to wear most days, and why? What are the other "props" you place around you in this portrait of you being completely fulfilled and successful?

This Gift Allows You to Choose Your Own Input

Is all of that important? Yes, it is. Everything you surround yourself with will influence your thoughts, your attitude, and your day in some way. If everything around you

35

influences and helps to program your mental computer, good or bad, what are the influences, the programmers, that you will choose to allow into your life?

The gift of surrounding yourself with success goes far beyond just choosing your friends—it alerts you to the importance of personally choosing everything in your life, right now, that is giving messages to your unconscious mind every moment of every day. Those messages, the subtle ones that you get from everything around you, have a tremendous impact on everything you think and everything you do. And they *will* play a vital role in your personal growth and in your success.

So, along with finding the *people* that enrich your life, choose a world that lifts you up, makes you feel good about yourself, and gets you ready for even greater things to come. If you want to be more successful in your business and have more fun and more positives in your life, surround yourself with the best—surround yourself with success.

And you can make that your *choice*.

Chapter 4

The Gift of *Choice*

T he gift of making choices for yourself is so important that I once wrote an entire book about it. By the book's conclusion, it was clear that it isn't the big choices we make that have the greatest impact on our lives; it's usually the smallest choices we make that affect us the most.

Of course, big choices—like where to live, who to marry, or what career you want—are life-directing choices. But so are choices like what time you get up in the morning, which friends you spend the most time with, what you eat, whether you write goals, and how many hours a day the TV is on.

It's often the seemingly most insignificant choices we

make each *day* that determine whether or not we succeed in *life*. And therein lies both the problem—and the *solution*.

Most of the Choices We *Think* We Make— We Don't Really Make

We can go through an entire day making dozens of choices, and never once *think* about the choices we're making. (We can actually arrive at work and not even remember the drive, or having driven there.) What we're *really* doing is just going along with habit, or with our old programming, and going through the day on auto-pilot, never pausing often enough to evaluate whether any one of those choices is really the best choice to make. We're *used* to doing it that way; why should we have to stop and *think* about it?

But when you consider what's really happening when you *don't* think about each choice you're making, that's kind of scary. If doing whatever it is you're doing is "the way you've always done it"—but at the same time, you'd like to change your life for the better—isn't it just possible you're working against yourself? Couldn't it be possible that some of your not-thought-about-too-much choices are *exactly* the wrong choices? (How would we know, if they're "automatic" choices and we never really think about them?)

The 100 Most Important Choices You Will Ever Make

In the book I wrote on making choices, I included a list of 100 of the most important choices we will ever make. What those 100 choices have in common is that, at first glance, most of them *seem* to be *insignificant*. Things like who you talk to on the telephone and how long you talk, whether you're usually on time when you're going somewhere, what kind of books you read, or what you do with your time off.

The message of that sample list of choices I included in that book is revealing, and I'll share a few of those choices with you here. As you read the list, think about your own life and keep in mind that, whether it might appear to be or not, *everything* on this list is a *choice*:

Who you spend most of your time with

What your favorite foods are

How often you call home

What books you read

How often or how seldom you smile

What you watch on TV and how much you watch

Your hobbies

How much you exercise

The style and color of the clothes you wear

Which telephone calls you return

The appearance of your home

How long something stays broke before you fix it

How late you stay up at night and why

What time you get up in the morning

How well you listen to others

How much risk you're willing to take

How you handle your money

Whether you are a leader or a follower

How calm you are

How interested you are in other people

How much time you take, just for yourself

Whether you give free advice

The kind of car you drive and what shape it's in

What sports you participate in

How much time you spend talking to your mate

How much money you have in your bank account

How you use credit cards

How important you feel you are

How you deal with problems

Who or what upsets you and why

How much patience you have

What you do when you don't get your way

How often you criticize someone else

How you feel about what other people think of you

How you take care of yourself

How much you respect yourself

How often you complain

How much encouragement you give to others

What you think about most

What you choose to get done today

That's just a partial list of the kinds of choices you make *that actually count the most.* Those are the kinds of choices that *literally* control your life. Every day.

The choice to select your career path, as an example, may be important, but it's what you *do* with that career path that will end up making your life filled with days of rewarding fulfillment—or days of endless drudgery, with you *living* only on weekends and wishing Monday would never come.

What that list should suggest to you is that it *is* the little choices that count the most. And *you* are in control of those choices—or at least you *should* be.

Unconscious Choices, Life-Changing Results

The problem with most of the choices we make, like the seemingly incidental choices on that list, is that most of them are *unconscious* choices—we make them, every day, without thinking about the fact that we're making them.

What happens is that our everyday choices in life are usually made by the unconscious programs we have that silently direct our lives for us. If we have great programs, the kind that automatically always steer us toward success, we're fortunate.

But all too often, our old programs steer us toward something *less* than what we could have been. At the time, we're too busy just living our lives to think about it. So our old programs, like the programs on a computer, do what they're designed to do. They make our multitude of daily *unconscious* choices *for* us.

The idea of that has always concerned me. It is as though instead of taking control of the most important choices in our lives in what we do with each day, we end up turning some of our most important daily choices over to our unconscious programming, which all too often, leads us in the wrong direction.

This Gift Has the Power to Change Almost *Everything*

When you begin taking the time to consciously think about the unconscious choices you make in your life each day, it's easy to see why this gift has the power to change almost *everything*.

The basic choice of what time you decide to get up in the morning, for example, can have a profound effect not only on your day, but also on your entire year. Likewise, the simple choice of who you call on the telephone every phone call you make, and why, can make the difference between launching your success—or just wasting time.

The most important message this gift gives you is that most of the choices you make each day are actually *yours* to make. Knowing that, and choosing to exercise your right to make those choices for yourself, gives you an incredible amount of freedom and control in a life that often seems to be over-controlled by the world around us.

During a break in a seminar I was conducting on "Choices," a woman came up to me, clearly in the midst of an astonishing breakthrough, and said at high volume, "It's *me!* It's *me!* *I'm* the one who's *responsible!* . . . It's *me!*" That woman, perhaps for the first time in her life, had just figured out the truth about her own *choices.* She got it. She finally understood that her choices were up to *her.* Where she was in her *life* was up to her.

Your own "aha" on this one may not be that dramatic or humorous, but the fact is, she was right. There is no *"they"* out there who can or should make our choices for us. We sometimes *think* that "they" (the world around us) set our schedules for us, tell us what we *ought* to do, and expect us to get in step with an agenda that *they* created for us. But the only person who should ever make your choices for you is *you.* The real "they" is *you.*

If You Want to "Succeed," Make Your Choices— *All* of Your Choices—For Yourself

That doesn't mean you shouldn't ever listen to your mate or take counsel with people you respect and trust. (Many times, as in a relationship, we make choices as joint choices, but what *we* choose is still up to us.) Get the advice and input you need. But then, always take counsel with yourself. Ask yourself what you really want to do next. Then make the best, *conscious*, well-thought-out choice you can make, and act on it. That's taking responsibility for yourself. That's putting *you* in control of your own life.

That also means that what happens next in your own life is up to you. What you consciously *choose* to do each day will make the difference between finding fulfillment and personal growth and achievement, or just going along with the life you were "given," and leaving your dreams behind.

It is a truth of personal growth, that you can only find true fulfillment when *you* take the lead in determining your own future. You may be surrounded by good people, a loving family, and other people who care. But you can only find the confidence and sense of accomplishment that comes from doing it yourself if you make the choices that count in your life each day—and make those choices for yourself. No one else should be allowed to do that for you.

A Role Model for Creating Personal Growth That Leaves Your Personal Choices Up to You

I said that I chose the Arbonne organization as a positive role model for personal growth because they practice a style of helping people live better lives—by guiding and encouraging them to do everything they can to live up to their best.

But if you're a member of that organization now, or if you study it carefully, you'll find that one thing Arbonne never does is tell you what choices *you* should make in your *own* life. They may give you helpful guidance and support, but they leave your personal choices up to you.

That's not only a sign of a company that understands people and cares about them, that's a great example of the kind of leadership that puts the ultimate responsibility of personal growth back where it belongs. They give you the tools you need to do almost anything with your life you could imagine—and I've seen many examples of that. But they leave the choices of what you'll do with those tools, and the choices of what you do with your life, firmly in your own capable hands.

"I'm Not at All Surprised My Life Is Working Better Now."

A perfect example of that is Shannon, an Arbonne consultant who told me that for the first time in her professional life, her choices are finally her own.

"In my old job, before Arbonne," Shannon said, "I didn't realize it at the time, but most of my choices were being made *for* me by someone else: what time I had to be somewhere, what I did with every hour of every day at work and sometimes outside of work, and usually even who I had lunch with. And all of those choices were for the benefit of someone else, the company I was working for. Not any more."

Shannon went on to tell me she had never realized how *much* of her previous life was being chosen for her by others. "I'm not at all surprised my life is working better now. I'm finally making progress. I'm making my choices for myself. No wonder I wasn't reaching my goals before! No wonder it was going so slow."

Shannon now spends her time working for her own future and for her family's future—instead of someone else's. Now *she's* making the choices that count.

What Are the Choices You Will Make Next?

When you read the list of even a few of the "100 Most Important Choices" I shared with you earlier, you may have found yourself thinking of the choices you make, or the choices you might want to make differently.

To find out what some of your choices might look like *if you thought about each of them first*, read the following list of questions—all of them choices—and listen closely for your answers:

What time will you get up tomorrow?

How will you spend your time during your day?

What goals will you work on?

Who will you spend most of your time with?

If you have a problem, will you worry about it, or will you work at it and solve it?

What will you do with the time you have to yourself?

What will you allow to upset you or upset your day?

Will you complain, or be positive and move on?

What will you talk about most this week?

What will you think about most?

Will you criticize someone else, or will you understand?

Will you be where you need to be, when you need to be there?

Will you always be on time?

Will you actively listen, instead of thinking of your own point of view?

What advice will you ask for, and whose advice will you take?

How often will you smile?

What kind of clothes will you wear?

How organized will you be?

How much time will you spend with your family?

How much time will you give to yourself?

What will you have for lunch?

What will you read?

What will you watch on television?

What is the last thing you'll choose to think about, just before you go to sleep tonight?

What is the first thing you'll think about, when you wake up in the morning?

The great truth of this gift is that *each* of us—and that means *you*—gets to make the choices that matter most. Each of us, no matter where we've been, what we've done before today, or where we are now, gets to make new choices. About *anything*. Every day.

That's an exhilarating thought. What an amazing realization it is to know that you get to *choose*. You get to make the choices that determine what you do with every moment of your day. Right now. Today. Tomorrow. And every day thereafter that you decide to choose.

You get to choose.

The world is made up of those who take control of their choices—and those who don't. Those who succeed use this tool every day they live, from the moment they find it.

What an incredible gift this tool is! *You get to make the choices that can change your life.*

The next gift not only helps other people around you, it makes you happier, feel better, and gives you rewards in every area of your life. It is the gift of helping other people grow.

Chapter 5

The Gift of Helping Other People Grow

T his gift gives you positive benefits in virtually every area of your life! It not only gives you a "guaranteed" way to build an incredible career, it gives you the kind of rewards you feel in your heart—the kind money can't buy.

It is a universal law of success that, when you help improve the lives of others, your *own* life will get better. If you want to succeed, help other people grow.

But now that same truth, in the form of one of the gifts, takes on an even greater importance. It's one thing to know you'd like to help other people improve their lives, but it's even better to know there is a practical way to actually make a positive impact on the life of virtually anyone you meet.

When I first began interviewing Arbonne consultants as part of my research, I noticed right away how many of them told me their greatest joy of being a consultant was that they were helping other people improve their lives.

Because they were introducing others to the Arbonne products, and then to Arbonne's positive business philosophy of personal growth, the consultants were finding that, as their own lives were showing marked improvements, so were the lives of the people who were joining them in the business. And the same story was taking place time and time again.

The Reward of Helping Other People Bring Their Dreams to Life

After months of continuing research and many more interviews, I was still hearing the same thing. It became clear that the results of Arbonne's philosophy of personal growth was changing a lot of lives.

Being an Arbonne consultant has given thousands of people many advantages—things like having money in the bank, the newfound freedom of being able to work for themselves from home, great new lifelong friends, greater self-worth, and a sense of personal security. But above all of these, as important as they are, the one reward spoken of most often by the consultants themselves is that of being able to help *other* people improve their lives.

Even people who may not start out in the business knowing that helping others would end up being one of their greatest rewards, soon find that the other lives they're changing are having a positive reflection in their *own* lives. As so many of the consultants have found, nothing else compares to the personal satisfaction and fulfillment of helping other people bring their dreams to life.

Get Ready For Your Life to Change

Let's take the experience of the many consultants I interviewed, and compare it to that universal law of success: *"When you help improve the lives of others, your own life will get better."*

If you wanted to find a shining example of the philosophy of "helping other people get better" in action, you would have to look no further than the personal story of almost any Arbonne consultant you met. And they're doing it every day.

That's pretty remarkable, considering there are many thousands of Arbonne people experiencing the same thing, and finding the same reward.

Of course, recognizing that there are several hundred million people on the planet who could use a little help—or a lot of help—there aren't, yet, enough Arbonne "life-changers" to go around. But when you're fortunate enough to meet one of them, make them a friend. And then get ready for your life to change.

The Reward Within

By the fact of that same universal law, when you help other people grow, you create important cause-and-effect results:

51

1. When you add value and purpose to someone else's life—you add more value and purpose to your *own* life.

This is one of those gifts that grows by the giving of it, and adds to your own life in many ways.

It is also one of those special gifts that you do not lose by giving it away. When you share it, the other person gets the gift, but you still get to keep it—and it grows.

Some years ago, when my own children were young, and I would read to them at night, I imagined that "giving" was like reading children a story out of a book when they were going to sleep. And I looked at it in a way I've never forgotten.

First, I imagined a world in which the words on the page could be read only once. Once you read the words to anyone, they would disappear from the page—like a gift that you lose when you give it to someone else.

But then, I imagined a world in which you could read the same story again and again, and the words would never disappear from the page; in fact, the story would get better every time it was shared.

Gifts of "self," like the gift of helping someone get better, are like the words of the story that—when you share it with someone else—you never lose from your life. And the story just keeps getting better.

2. When you help someone else get better, you increase your Self-Esteem.

This is a wonderful reward you receive for helping

someone else get better. When your self-esteem grows, so do you, in every positive way. You become more confident. You have less fear—because you can see your strengths more clearly. You're more willing to step forward and take good chances that help you grow in your own life. You accomplish more, you're more fulfilled as a person, and you open up to greater opportunities in front of you. So you do more and create more good. And when you're doing good things you feel better about yourself. And when you feel better about yourself you increase your self-esteem . . . and the positive cycle begins again.

3. When you help other people get better, you naturally and automatically learn and practice positive leadership traits.

Whether you started out wanting to be a "leader" or not, if you believe in others and you help them improve their lives, you become a leader.

Your "leadership" role may simply be the example you set. Or you may go beyond that, and more actively share your experiences and your progress with others. Or you may go to the next step, and "train" others, so they can learn what you've discovered. (The real meaning of the word "training" is "sharing.")

But whichever role you choose, when you help other people improve their lives, you will become, in a very natural way, a leader.

4. When you help other people get better, you expand your focus in life in many ways.

When you're actively helping other people improve their lives, your focus changes—from just you and your world, to *them* and *their* worlds. Your attitude takes a shift upwards. You "feel" the benefits you're creating in other people's lives, and your own daily zest and enthusiasm for living increases as a result. You move from being a "bystander" to someone who is "making a difference"—and you can *feel* the difference.

The result of that difference can be as subtle as what you choose to do tomorrow, or how you talk to people, to your relationship with your family getting better, or your own personal goals becoming clearer and your action steps more defined, so you're more sure about what to do next.

As a researcher and writer in the field of behavioral psychology, I've had the opportunity to observe the difference between lives that "work" and lives that don't; lives that are rich and fulfilling—and lives that are wanting or hurting. In the years that I've worked in this field, I've never found a single example of a truly "successful" person who was not actively practicing the principle of helping other people prosper, or get better. Your own successes are always tied in some way to the betterment you are helping to create in the lives of others.

If you're already one of those who knows the joy of helping others in your own life, you're probably already using this gift every day. If you're already an Arbonne consultant, you certainly have a story to share and a way to immediately help other people improve their well-being. If you're not already doing that, I hope you will, and watch what happens in your own life when you help other people *noticeably* improve their lives.

Can You Help Other People Get Better— If You're Not Where You Want to Be Yourself?

Never wait until you're perfect to help someone else get better. None of us will ever be perfect.

A woman I trained as a life coach wanted to help women with weight problems because she was overweight herself, and she had been fighting the battle for years. When she told me she was going to get started life coaching just as soon as she lost thirty pounds, I suggested that she not wait, but start life coaching immediately. I explained that she would solve her own weight problem faster by helping other people solve theirs, and that's exactly what happened. Had she waited to start life coaching until she was the "perfect" weight herself, she would probably still be waiting.

Kristina, one of the Arbonne consultants I interviewed, had a chronic skin condition when she first became a consultant, and she was worried that her own appearance would cause people to question her story of how good skin care can improve your appearance.

She went ahead with her Arbonne business anyway, and had immediate success with her friends' complexions when they started using the Arbonne products. Meanwhile, Kristina and her own complexion started to take on a different tone. As she told me later, "I'm glad I started when I did. I got encouragement from the friends I introduced the products to, my own skin cleared up, and now *I'm* my one of my success stories."

Sharing good ideas with people isn't about where you are now. If each of us waited to help someone else until we were totally on top ourselves, we would never get started. Wherever you are in your life, if you want to help other people grow, *now* is a good time to begin.

Chapter 6

The Gift of Believing in Yourself

T here is no greater personal strength you can ever have, other than faith itself, than the strength of *self-belief*—the gift of *believing* in yourself.

Without self-belief we hesitate—or never move at all. When we do not believe in ourselves, we cannot believe in our future—so we have no vision. And without vision, we have no dream. Without a dream we no plan. Without a plan there is no accomplishment. And without accomplishment, there is no reward. So, without self-belief, there is no fulfillment.

It all begins with believing in yourself.

When we *have* strong self-belief, the achievement is already almost won. *With* self-belief we eagerly step forward into each new day, confident in the positive outcome of anything we do. *With* self-belief, we open our arms to the bright future that awaits us. *With* self-belief, we have *faith*, not just in ourselves, but in every tomorrow in front of us.

Without self-belief, we can't even see tomorrow clearly, —and with it, we can see forever. With self-belief, we find the best of ourselves. We find fulfillment—and the best of the life we're living.

Finding the Self-Belief You Need

If having strong, healthy self-belief is that important—and it *is*—then it's clear that none of us could ever have too much of it. The stronger our self-belief, the better we do.

But how is it that some people come to have plenty of self-belief, while others seem to have so little of it? If you have some self-belief, can you get more of it? Or if you have only a little self-belief, can you somehow get enough of it to succeed in life the way other people do?

Self-belief is not something that's carefully doled out to some, but not to others. It's not some kind of "magic blessing" that's given to a few—and withheld from everyone else. The *results* of having exceptional self-belief might seem like a miracle, but getting self-belief to start with is *not*. We get it naturally.

That's good news. That means no matter how much or how little you believe in yourself right now, you can get as much self-belief as you need. And you can get it naturally—just like other people got theirs in the first place.

So let me reassure you. If you'd like to have more self-belief, you can get more. By the end of this chapter, I'll show you how.

The *Real* Kind of Self-Belief

We're not talking here about the kind of self-assessment that makes you think you're completely self-sufficient, above God, or better than others. *True* self-belief is the *opposite* of that. It's when you live up to the promise of your best, God-given potential that you create worthwhile results and benefits in every area of your life, and for everyone around you as well.

True self-belief should never be mistaken for self-pride or arrogance. Wholesome, positive self-belief is an expression of our acceptance of the talents and the potential we were born with, to put to good use in our lives.

That is, indeed, a great gift—one we should be thankful to have. And one we should do everything in our power to bring to life.

The Kind of Self-Belief You Got
While Growing Up

There are two ways in which our self-belief comes to us.

Our first sense of self-belief came from the programs we received while we were growing up. From the time we were very young, if we were fortunate, we were taught to believe in ourselves by our parents or others around us. Some people were fortunate enough to get that kind of positive programming; others were not.

Children who receive consistent, positive reinforcement and belief from the people who raise them learn to believe in themselves because they're constantly shown what they *can* do, instead of being shown only what they *cannot* do. That's healthy early programming, and the results of that kind of programming can last for a lifetime.

A Series of Small Successes

The second way we build self-belief is through the repeated experience of small successes. Good grades at school can do that. Or doing well enough at some sport that you get the recognition from your coach and teammates that tells you you've got what it takes to win.

Anything you do that you put effort into, and then win in some way, gives you another success. When you continue to do that, you create the *habit* of success, and along with it, self-belief. That kind of self-belief can also last for a lifetime—far beyond school or athletics.

Something Someone Said to Us— or Something We Did for Ourselves

To simplify a very complex process in the human brain, we can say that almost all of the initial self-belief we got, came to us as a result of something someone said to us (*"You did* great!" "You have a lot of talent!" "You're really good at that."), or from something we did that we saw as successful, and then repeated those kinds of successes until they felt natural and automatic to us. In both of those cases, the positive input programmed us with self-belief. While we were young, we either got a lot of those kinds of programs, or we might not have gotten enough of them.

In either case, when you were growing up (and since that time), what you got is what you got. And that's how you ended up here—wherever you are today. So if you have incredible self-belief, say a great big "thank you" to your past experiences—your past programs—and feel good about it.

If, on the other hand, you weren't given as much self-belief as you should have gotten, say a "thank you" for the fact that you made it this far anyway, and feel good about the fact that you *now* get to have just as much self-belief as you *want*.

Creating Self-Belief for *Yourself*

People have asked me, "How can I suddenly believe in myself, if I don't really believe in myself?" I understand what seems to be the paradox in that. But it only appears to be one.

The truth is, if you want to have more self-belief now, you don't have to *start* by believing in yourself. You have to start by getting some new *programs*, and by doing a few things differently. Here's how it works.

Your early self-belief was the result of two things: receiving positive messages about you, and you creating your own self-confidence by repeating actions that worked for you. Now, as a grown-up, you build self-belief today in exactly those same ways—through positive *"input"* (by getting strong, new, healthy programs of self-belief) and through accomplishing tasks and doing them well—but this time you're consciously and actively creating that self-belief for yourself.

Seven Exercises for Building Self-Belief

If you don't always have strong self-belief, or would like to have more of it, here are seven exercises that will help you.

1. Start by getting new programs that build your self-belief.

This is an essential first step to building self-belief. When you were growing up, you either got the right programs, or you didn't get enough of them. If you didn't, you can do something about that.

In the next chapter we'll talk about Self-Talk, and how to change your old programs. I'll show you how to do that.

2. Make a list of the things you are most proud of having done.

What are some of the things you've done in your life that you're most proud of? What are some of them that immediately come to mind? For this exercise, I'd like you to write an actual list out on paper. Go as far back as you can, and include everything you've done that you felt especially good about.

There's a reason for this exercise. Most of us have done better than we think we've done. But negative doubts often override the positive truths, so we forget the best of who we are. Writing the list will help you remember the things you did that worked. (Most people who lack self-belief are much better than they think they are.)

3. Schedule two or three small tasks that challenge you—but ones you know you can accomplish if you work at them—and get them done in the next week.

Because we learn greater self-belief by creating a series of small successes, it will also work for you to do that now, when you'd like to build your self-belief.

Find a few things that you can accomplish, but that represent a minor challenge to you, and one by one, complete each one of them within the next week. This can be something as simple as making an appointment with the doctor or organizing your schedule and finding the time to do something you've been putting off doing. Accomplishment is created in small steps. And accomplishment, no matter how small, builds self-belief.

At the end of the week, schedule three or four more tasks and complete them during week two. Then, do the same thing again for a third one-week period. At the end of just those three weeks, you may be positively surprised at the improvement in your self-belief. (And you'll have gotten a lot of things done, at the same time.)

4. Each week for the next three weeks, accept at least one larger challenge you've been avoiding and get it done.

Unlike the small-challenge tasks above, in this exercise, choose a challenge each week that you either fear or avoid, and tackle it. Think of something you've been avoiding. Then set a goal to get it done now. Deal with it. Look straight at it, *do* it, keep breathing, and watch what happens.

5. Avoid, completely, saying or thinking anything *negative* about yourself at any time or for any reason.

As you may already know, your own thoughts, if they're negative (even the quietest doubts), can be your greatest enemy. What you *say* about you, and what you *think* about you, will have more to do with your belief in yourself than anything else you do.

We'll talk more about this, also, in the next chapter, but beginning now, make a deal with yourself: always, in every case, in everything you think and say about you, show yourself the *best* about you. (If you can't believe the best about everything you've done in the past, you can still believe in the best about everything you'll do in the future.) If you keep doing that, you'll start to believe it—which is exactly what you ought to be doing.

When you always believe the *best* about yourself—in time, the *best* is what you'll always get.

6. Ignore the negative opinions of others.

Starting immediately, from now on, *always and forever* ignore the negative opinions of people around you. Whether they're family, friends, acquaintances, in-laws, or people at work—ignore *anyone* who has a negative thought of any kind, about you. Walk away—or tune them out. Smile and feel good! And think great thoughts about yourself. Don't give the other person a second thought. You have far more positive things to do with your mind—and your life.

Always keep in mind that when it comes to anyone's appraisal of you (or your own appraisal of yourself), there is *no* negative opinion that counts. Ignoring forever the negative opinions of others is a great exercise for building self-belief. Tuning out the negatives, or walking away, will become a habit that shouts to you from within, *"I believe in myself. I like who I am, and I'm glad to be me!"*

Every time you do that, you win! (You also immediately improve your self-esteem.)

7. Find those who *believe* in you completely, and listen to *their* words of positive truth about you.

Listen to the people who show you the *best* of yourself. Listen to the right people, the ones who tell you the good about you, every chance you get. Just as you can choose to *avoid* the opinions of people who are negative and defeating, choose to *share* your time with people whose words are uplifting and believing. Those people may seem to be harder to find, but all it takes is the right few.

And when those people show you a positive picture of you, make a deal with yourself: when you hear something good

65

about yourself, *listen* to it. Don't doubt it, don't deny it, and don't dispute it. Just *accept* it—with grace. And *believe* it.

"I Didn't Know I Could Learn How to Believe in Myself Again."

A lot of people grow up with some measure of self-belief, but then, through a bad relationship or life's misfortunes, they lose the self-belief they once had.

One Arbonne consultant named Jennifer related to me that she was raised with strong self-belief and self-esteem, but later, problems in her marriage and a husband who had little or no self-belief of his own, began to erode her belief in herself.

"I had really worked hard to keep myself positive," Jennifer told me, "but after awhile, the negative things can wear you down. Eventually, even after trying very hard," Jennifer said, "there was not much of the real me left."

It was after that, that Jennifer was introduced to Arbonne, and became a consultant herself. With the help of a new goal and the support and belief of other Arbonne consultants, she began to find her "real" self again. Over a period of months (it didn't happen overnight), Jennifer found that her life, and her marriage, took on a new, more promising direction. She began to find her self again, and along with that, a new sense of self-belief.

Some two years later, I interviewed Jennifer, and I don't think I would have recognized the doubtful Jennifer of two years earlier. What she told me was inspiring when she said, "I didn't know I could learn to believe in myself again. But I did. I got myself back, better than ever, and I'll never lose myself again."

She had it back—and then some! And her life story had changed immeasurably—for the better—in the process. Her marriage was working, her new career was working, and her *life* was working. She had found the self-belief she had lost.

I could credit Jennifer's new-found life to the support she got from some very caring Arbonne associates who helped her take a giant step forward in a time of crisis—and they certainly did that. But I credit Jennifer herself with making the choice to bring herself back and *believe in herself* once again. She had just found the right place to do it.

Create a Moment of *"Instant Self-Belief"*

Wherever you are in your life right now, if you'd like to create some additional self-belief, I'd like to suggest a very effective idea for you to try.

This is fun to do. And when it works for you, I think you'll agree that it proves just how quickly you can bring your self-belief to life.

What we're going to do is create a moment of "Instant Self-Belief." You can use this technique no matter *what's* happening at the moment. It could be anything from being pulled over by a traffic cop to having to get up in front of a group and make a presentation. Or it could be when someone is angry with you, or when you're about to make a difficult telephone call. You can do this *anytime*.

What You Tell Yourself *Next*
Can Change Everything

At that moment, just as you feel the anxiety hit, like that sudden clutch in your stomach—at that moment, *stop*. Whatever you're thinking, stop. Wipe your mind clear. Ignore the blinking red and blue lights in your rear-view mirror. Just erase them for the moment.

Or if you're about to get up in front of that group to speak, just erase them for a few seconds.

And in that moment, see yourself literally *beaming* in the happiest, most successful, most on-top-of-it, "perfect moment" photograph you can put in your mind. If you have an actual photograph you can picture in your mind, put it there. If you have to create one in your mind, have one ready in advance and put it there.

Now, in that same moment, as you're seeing that absolutely incredible on-top-of-the-world picture of yourself, immediately tell yourself the following:

"I believe in myself, I believe in myself, I believe in myself! I can do this! I'm on top, in tune, in touch, and going for it! Today is my day, and nothing can stop me now. I believe in myself, and I'm doing great! Now is my time. I'm glad to be alive. I'm glad to be here! And I'm just getting started!"

Say that to yourself instantly, and say it with *vigor*. Say it with intensity and with absolute certainty!

In that moment, you become the "Little Engine That *Could*." (Or the big, grownup person that could.)

Will creating a moment of "Instant Self-Belief" change

your day when you need it most? Yes, it will. Why? Because when you see that incredible picture of you, and say those kinds of words with strength and enthusiasm, you deliver to your unsuspecting brain a *powerful* message—a *barrage* of chemicals that will tell your brain to go into ***"high energy positive mode."*** And when it does, you'll feel it—instantly!

You can do that anytime. You can try it right now, in fact. Go outside, get that super-positive picture of you in your mind, open your arms wide and shout at the sky, *"I believe in myself! Today is my day! And nothing can stop me now!"*

Try *that* the next time your self-belief is wavering. Or the next time you're being pulled over by a traffic cop. And let me know what happens.

You Can *Do* it, and You *Know* You Can

Believing in yourself, then, really gets down to two things. One is to become *aware* of your own self-belief, all the time, and to actively follow the steps to build it—by improving your old programs with new Self-Talk, avoiding the negatives of others, and practicing having a lot of small successes. Be aware of it, work at it and build it.

The other is to practice *having* self-belief—like employing the idea of having "Instant Self-Belief" anytime you want it, and doing that a lot. Make the words *"I believe in myself"* a part of your automatic mental vocabulary and use them every day. That does sound simple, and almost too easy. But that's the way the best ideas of personal growth always work.

As you're practicing self-belief, you'll find that bigger and bigger success moments, and bigger successes, will naturally start to happen. That's the way it works.

One of the Most Important Choices You Will Ever Make—and You Can Make it Right Now

The wonderful truth of self-belief is this: for the rest of your life, *the choice to believe in yourself* is entirely up to you. You get to believe in yourself anytime you want. (How about right now?)

Believing in yourself—from here onward—isn't up to your past programming; it isn't up to where you've been or what you've done up to now; it's not up to the rest of the world; it's not up to the other people around you, and it's not up to whatever circumstances you might find yourself in right now.

Imagine waking up tomorrow morning, and saying to yourself, *"I believe in myself."* Say it over a few times, and mean it. *"I believe in myself. I believe in myself. I believe in myself."* And then, go ahead . . . *believe in yourself.*

When you do that, you're going to have a better day. And when you're having a good day, and you believe in yourself, just *imagine* what you can do *next*.

Now we come to one of the most exciting and most life-changing personal growth tools that has ever been discovered. It is the gift of changing your programs by changing your Self-Talk, and it is a gift you can use for the rest of your life.

Chapter 7

The Gift of Changing Your Self-Talk

I f you want to change your life and make it better, there is one thing you can do that all successful people do: you can change your self-talk.

There are tens of thousands of people who now use a *new* kind of Self-Talk every day, and their lives are changing—often dramatically for the better—because of it. In fact, today, the concept of Self-Talk is changing millions of lives all over the world.

Among the millions who have learned to use the gift of Self-Talk, not surprisingly, are tens of thousands of Arbonne consultants who have changed their futures by changing their Self-Talk. Many of them were introduced to the concept of Self-Talk for the first time by one of their associates in the business, or through Arbonne's ongoing training program.

It was there that many of the consultants first learned that important call to attention about their own past programming:

"Change your Self-Talk and you will change your programs. Change your programs and you will change your life."

When You *Change* Your Self-Talk, You Change Your *Life*

When people discover the truth about how we get programmed, often in the wrong way, and how our programs direct and affect almost everything in our lives, it can, at first, look like life itself is working against us. If we are living our lives with programs that are harmful or negative—if we have the *wrong* programs—what chance do we have?

Fortunately, there's more than hope; there's a solution that works. Self-Talk is one of the gifts, one of those major secrets of life, that once we "get it," can change almost everything for us. When you get *this* gift, when you figure it out and apply it in your own life, you will open doors to your future that you might have otherwise thought impossible.

So to understand this gift, and to use it for yourself, it will help you to know that it is a gift that will turn the *negative* to the *positive*, the *bad* to the *good*, and the *impossible* to the *possible*. By the end of this chapter, I think you'll know what I mean.

The Secret of *"Self-Talk"* Brings the *Best* of Ourselves Back to *Life*

One personal example of this is a woman by the name of Liz. Liz is an Arbonne consultant who was scheduled to receive a new car (a beautiful white Mercedes) for having reached the level of Regional Vice President in her Arbonne business. Liz had worked hard and earned the reward, but she credited her discovery of Self-Talk as the reason she had done so well in her business as an Arbonne consultant.

One of Liz's upline mentors had recommended to her the first book I wrote on Self-Talk, entitled *"What To Say When You Talk To Your Self,"* and Liz had taken the book to heart, learned how to change her Self-Talk, and in turn, changed a lot of her attitudes and her actions.

I learned about this when I got a phone call from Rita Davenport (who, you'll recall, is the incredibly caring president of Arbonne). Rita told me that Liz's sponsor wanted to give her an *extra* gift, along with the car, when she received the keys to her new Mercedes at an award ceremony to be held in a few weeks.

Liz, I learned, had not only told her entire team how the powerful concept of Self-Talk had turned her career around; she had even gone so far as to have cards imprinted with special, positive Self-Talk phrases, to be placed on the tables at everyone's seat at the upcoming awards presentation.

Since Liz was telling the story of Self-Talk so strongly, her sponsor thought it would be a great surprise to have me phone Liz, live on stage during the event. So Rita asked me if I would be willing to make a special phone call to Liz during the presentation of her new car.

73

I was humbled by the request, but I felt privileged to personally congratulate one of my book readers who had clearly "gotten it" and had put Self-Talk into practice in her life and in her business.

When the night of the presentation came, Liz, on stage, had just been given a beautifully framed copy of the book I had written, *"What To Say When You Talk To Your Self,"* when a telephone, on stage, rang—and it was a call for a very surprised Liz. Both ends of our phone conversation had been piped through the PA system in the room, so everyone could hear my personal congratulations to Liz for being an incredible achiever. I was told later that, after seeing Liz on stage that evening, there wasn't a dry eye in the audience. It was quite an evening for all of us.

I met Liz, in person, a short time later, and found her to be an outstanding example of what someone can do when they make the choice to change their Self-Talk, change their programs, and change their life. Liz told me that before she discovered Self-Talk, her successes in life had been on hold in every way, and she was reaching *none* of her goals. But *since* she started practicing the right Self-Talk, she has become unstoppable in her Arbonne business, and in finding fulfillment in the rest of her life as well.

All of Us Get Programmed

The Self-Talk book that was recommended to Liz was an earlier book of mine about how *all* of us get *programmed* as children growing up, and how those programs end up determining most of what we do with the rest of our lives.

When I wrote that book, personal computers were not as popular as they are today. The world then was just learning the relationship between everything we type into our computers, the "input," and what our computers give us back—the "output."

We had already learned the term "GIGO," the acronym for "garbage in, garbage out." It was an early, somewhat clumsy way of saying that whatever we type *into* a computer is exactly what we will get back *out* of it.

When the computer scientists coined the phrase GIGO, they were talking only about *computer* programming. At the time, they had no idea how close they had come to defining the programming process of *another* kind of computer—the *human brain.*

Our Very Personal On-Board Computer

A human being isn't a computer, of course. The mind of a human being is a complex, biochemical miracle that still confounds the greatest computer scientists. But the human brain *does* operate in many ways like the computers that were patterned after it. And from the science of computer technology, we have learned a great lesson about the human mind: *Whatever you put into it is exactly what you will get back out of it.*

From the First Moments of Our Lives . . .

Imagine that we're standing outside the window in the

75

newborn nursery at the hospital, and gazing in wonder at the infants that lie within.

As we're watching, we notice one baby in particular, lying there, nestled in her little bassinet, precious and waiting. She's a *beautiful* child, in every way. Along with love and warmth and security, her small, infant, undefined mind is waiting for every *input* her new life is about to give her.

It is as though she has a tiny computer keyboard strapped to her little infant chest, waiting for all of us older, wiser humans to type in the words, and the messages, and the pictures of the future that we're about to give her. From that moment forward, everything we say, everything we do— every message we give her, in any way—will be programmed into her eagerly waiting, open mind.

Children aren't computers, of course. They're warm, wonderful little human beings, born with incredible potential, just waiting for the right messages and the right programs to be typed into their little keyboards. But the truth is, the programming process is very much the same in our *mental* computers—as in the computers on our desks.

That's Where Our Future Begins

Each of *our* lives began as an infant with unlimited potential, waiting for the right programs—the right messages. As we grew older, some of us got good messages, and some of us did not. For most of us, it was a mixture of both.

But whatever programs we got, whatever they were, our young computer-like brains took them in, and recorded them—all of them—in the vast computer storage centers of our subconscious minds.

What behavioral scientists did not know, until recently, was that our computer brains were designed not only to *store* all of the input we got, but also to *act* on those programs as though they were *true*. The result is that you and I, today, *think*, *believe*, and *act* based on the programming we received, as though the programs we received were *true*—whether they were true or not.

How Self-Talk Works

Here's how it works, and why our new understanding of Self-Talk and programming is important to your own life:

From the moment you were born, everything that has ever been said to you, everything you have ever heard, seen, done, or experienced has been programmed into the storage center of your brain—your subconscious mind. Every "message" you have received has been typed into your computer storage banks. Permanently.

All of the thoughts and messages that were typed into your computer along the way are still there. Good, bad, or otherwise, the programs you received, first as a small child, then as a teenager, and then as an adult, are still with you today, recorded and stored, chemically and electrically, word for word, in the neural networks of your brain.

Our Brain Stores the Messages We Get—
As Though They're *True*

77

The most important revelation is that the part of the brain that stores all of these messages for us (like a giant filing cabinet) doesn't know the difference between something that is *true or false, bad or good, positive or negative.* It just takes the messages in, stores them, and *acts* on them as though they're *true*.

The result of this is that who we are, or who we *believe* ourselves to be, is based on the programs we have stored about ourselves in our subconscious minds. It doesn't make any difference if the programs we got were false or inaccurate programs. Our brain today, dealing with what it believes to be the so-called "truths" about us—that it has stored in its files—simply *acts* on the programs it has to work with, whether they're true or not.

Here are some examples of the kinds of things some parents have said to their children—without ever realizing that they're actually typing *permanent* programs into their children's wide open, eagerly waiting computer minds:

"You're so clumsy, you could never be a ballerina."

"Sometimes I think you don't have a brain in your head."

"You're going to grow up to be chubby just like your Aunt Harriet."

"Who do you think you are, someone special?"

"Can't you do anything right?"

"Your room is always a mess."

"All you do is talk back."

78

"Why should I trust you?"

"You'll be the death of me yet!"

"I wish you'd never been born."

"You never tell the truth."

"You're just like your father!" (Said only when a child has done something wrong.)

"You're impossible!"

"You're so stupid!"

"You'll just mess it up."

"Why can't you be more like your sister?"

"You just don't think!"

"You'll never amount to anything!"

"What makes you think you're so smart?"

"You never listen when I talk to you."

"You think home is just a place to sleep."

"You never shut up."

"I can't believe a word you say."

"You're the laziest person I've ever seen."

"Everything I say to you goes in one ear and out the other!"

"Girls are no good at math."

"You should be ashamed of yourself."

"You're just thirteen, you don't know anything!"

"You'd lose your head if it wasn't screwed on."

"You don't have the talent."

"I think your brother got the brains."

"You might as well not try, it's not going to work out anyway."

. . . and on, and on, and on.

The Story of a Girl Named Kimberly

Let's imagine we know a young teenage girl who has repeatedly been given programs like those. Maybe not all of those programs, but some of them. Her name is Kimberly.

After enough of that kind of negative programming over a few years, if we asked Kim to describe herself, her description could, unfortunately, sound something like this:

"I'm clumsy, I don't have a brain in my head, I never do anything right, I'll always be overweight and I'm going to grow up to be fat, I'm not organized, my room is always a mess, I'm lazy, I'm always late, I have no talent, I'm ashamed of myself, I'm not special, I don't tell the truth, I talk back, I never listen, I'm not good at anything, I wish I'd never been born, I'll never amount to anything, and it's no use even trying—I know it won't work anyway."

In describing herself, Kim has unconsciously *repeated* the

programs she got *most*—and her subconscious mind now believes them to be *true!*

What if Kim really believes that *that's* the way she really *is*? Kim may not be perfect, but because of the programs she's gotten over and over again, she now *believes* she's already a failure! And she's just *thirteen* years old! She hasn't even *begun* to *live* her life and find her *promise*.

What if *Kimberly* was the little infant we saw in the nursery in the hospital earlier, waiting for her own future to come to life? What if that infant with *unlimited* potential was *Kim*?

If that beautiful little infant we saw was Kimberly, just a few short years ago, *what have we done?*

We Are Seldom Even *Aware* of the Programs That Lead Us Through Our Lives

An even more troubling aspect of Kim's story is that most of the beliefs she has about herself are *unconscious*. For now, and for most of her life, like *ours*, the programs that direct her are *invisible*. She can't see them for herself. But they're just as strong, and they'll do just as much to direct her life (or *mis*direct it) as they would if they were printed in bold letters on cards that she carried around with her and read out loud to herself every day.

For Most of Us, the *"No's"* Outweighed the *"Yes's"*

The list of negative messages that Kim got, is just a sample of the kinds of early life programs many of us received when we were young. There are hundreds more messages just like them. And then we get more of the same, and sometimes *worse*, from the *rest* of the world around us.

All of us, growing up, got too many programs like that. Even if we grew up in fairly positive homes, we got the messages. It's been estimated that during the first eighteen years of our lives, the average individual is told "no" or what we "cannot" do, or what we've done "wrong," more than *148,000 times*!

(Wouldn't you rather have heard how good, or talented, or smart, or special, or capable, or successful, or loved you were?)

Our Programs Come From Everywhere Around Us

Beyond the programs our parents gave us—when they were usually just trying to protect us—the *rest* of the world stepped in and fed us *more* pictures of us that were often negative or less than the best. Many of the programs kids get from television, as an example, aren't just negative; they're menacingly *destructive*.

Not all of the programs we received were bad, of course. Some of the programs we got were good. But behavioral researchers have told us that as much as *77%* of all of the programs we received are *negative, false, counter-productive, or work against us!*

Simple Words and Messages Create Programs
That *Stay* with Us for a *Lifetime*

As an example of this, the simple words, *"Are you sure you're feeling all right?"* spoken only on those occasions when a child clearly looks ill, would not create a negative health "program." But the same or similar message, repeated again and again by an over-protective parent, especially when the child is *fine*, and probably healthy, can create negative health programs that will last a lifetime.

I knew a girl in school when I was young, named Carole Ann. Every time I saw them together, Carole Ann's mother constantly said the same things to her daughter—things like, *"You look a little faint, are you sure you're feeling all right?"* or *"Why don't you just rest a little while, dear, you look like you're not feeling too well,"* or *"Carole Ann, sweetheart, are you sure you're not coming down with something?"*—when there was *nothing* at all wrong with Carole's health. (The only time the mother touched her daughter was on her forehead to see if she had a fever.)

I noticed that eventually, with enough negative programming from her un-knowing mother, Carole Ann actually *was* starting to frequently become ill. During the next few years at school, I think Carole Ann missed more days of school due to "sickness" than any of her classmates. Was she really in poor health? Not at all—at least not at first.

I've often wondered what would have happened to Carole Ann if her mother had constantly told her what a *healthy* girl she was and how *vibrant* she looked. I suspect that she would have almost *never* been sick or missed school.

Without Us Even Thinking About It, Our *Programs* Take Over and Direct Our Lives For Us

There are countless stories about how the people who program us can unknowingly steal our futures from us. It can be about *anything*.

I know people who will *always* be broke—if they do nothing about the fact that their *programs* are broke. Or people who can't seem to make a relationship work, because their programs tell them they're not good enough, or that they're just naturally bad at relationships.

Many people who struggle with weight do so because their programs, to this day, tell them that just one more little bite of the comfort food in front of them won't hurt.

Other people never get *close* to achieving their childhood dreams because *their dreams were taken away from them* before they even had a *chance* to bring them to life!

Your Programs Shape Your Identity—and Determine Your Success

All of that is the result of the wrong messages, repeated often enough to make them stick. And when those programs win, *you* lose. Your attitudes, your skills, your creativity, the way you communicate, your career, your income, your relationships, how organized you are . . . *everything* about you is affected by those programs.

If you have ever struggled with negativity, fear, self-doubt, or failure, let me assure you, it wasn't "you"—it was your old

84

programs all along.

No matter what it's about, any program you receive often enough becomes a permanent part of your identity, and ends up telling you what you believe about yourself—and who you think you are—for the rest of your life.

The Parents Who *Know*—and the Parents Who *Don't*

There is a life-changing difference between parents who give their kids positive messages of growth and potential, and the opposite. The parent who understands this says things like, *"That's a good painting. You're really talented. If you wanted to, you could be a great artist someday!"*

Meanwhile, the parent who *doesn't* understand might thoughtlessly say, *"I don't know why you spend so much time drawing those silly pictures. You might have a little talent, but you're certainly never going to be a Picasso."*

Which of those two young kids, getting those kinds of repeated programs from their parents, do you suppose will express their talents and see them grow? Which of them will tuck their creativity away, stop expressing themselves artistically, and never see their potential blossom, and see the light of day?

Our Parents Did Their Best—They Just Gave Us the Same Kinds of Programs *They* Received

85

I'm not blaming parents, of course. They're just repeating the programs *they* got from *their* parents, and handing them down to the kids they're now raising. When they do that, they're not *trying* to limit their kids' lives—they're just giving their kids the programs *they* got when *they* were growing up.

The same is true of teachers at school, friends, other family members, and everyone else around us. They weren't trying to *intentionally* limit us and make us fail or get less than the best in our lives. Most of the people we meet in the world around us just don't *know*.

Through Our Own Self-Talk, We Unconsciously Repeat the Strongest Programs We Got

What happens after we get the programs we are given is that we begin to *unconsciously* repeat back to *ourselves* the same programs we got.

When that happens, our computer brain is only doing what it was *designed* to do. It plays those same exact programs *back* to us—repeatedly, again and again. And in the process, it creates our Self-Talk—the unconscious Self-Talk we have today—the powerful but unconscious messages and directions that dominate our thinking and direct our lives.

Simplifying a Complex Process

This is actually a chemical and electrical process in the brain. Medical science has discovered that what's happening neurologically when we're getting those messages is that the brain is *recording* them and storing them in an incredibly complex system of neural networks. Some program pathways are faint, not very strong. They're the pathways that received less input—fewer repeated messages.

Other program pathways are vibrant and strong, coursing with electrochemical energy. Those are the program pathways that got more activity—more messages repeated more often. The more often the same kind of program is *repeated*, recorded in the brain, the stronger it becomes. (The key to programming is repetition, repetition, repetition.)

What Does Your Own Self-Talk Sound Like Today?

In time, everything we *think*, what we *believe* about ourselves, the *choices* we make each day, and the *actions* we take, are all affected by those programs—the ones we got that were the strongest—the ones that were repeated most often.

All we have to do to see the results of those programs is to listen to our own Self-Talk now.

Just as we saw in the example of Kim's teenage self-talk—of the disbelieving, negative kind—here are just a few examples of the kinds of things we as adults end up saying and unconsciously accepting as truth, because it's what our computer brains have been programmed to believe.

In the examples below, I've listed just a few of the most obvious things we might hear people say, or things you may actually have said yourself. Here are some examples of the kind of self-talk phrases that work *against* us.

In your own life, from other people or from yourself, see

if you recognize any of these:

I can never remember names.

Nothing ever goes right for me.

I can never find anything.

That's just my luck.

Everything I eat goes right to my _____ (fill in the blank.)

Today just isn't my day!

I'm so clumsy.

I never have enough money left over at the end of the month.

I just hate to talk in front of a group.

I just can't do it.

I never seem to have enough energy.

Why even try?

I could never do that.

It's just no use.

I'm just not creative.

I can't seem to get organized!

I can never afford the things I want.

I'm too shy to do that.

I never know what to say.

Sometimes I just hate myself.

With my luck, I don't have a chance!

I never get a break.

I'm no good at math.

I'm nothing without my first cup of coffee in the morning.

I never seem to get anyplace on time.

I'm just not cut out for that.

I'm really at the end of my rope.

If only I were smarter.

If only I had more time.

If only I had more money.

. . . and the list goes on and on and on . . .

Did you find any of your own "past thinking" anywhere on that list? It's no surprise that many of the things we repeat to ourselves today are the *same* kinds of messages that thirteen-year-old Kim was using in her poorly programmed teenage description of herself. Now, years later, unless we do something about it, we still have the *same* programs—but over time, they've gotten *worse*.

You Can *Change* Your Programs
by Changing Your Self-Talk

What a wonderful, life-changing tool—what a wonderful *gift* this is! Just as Liz, who changed her Self-Talk and earned the Mercedes, and a whole lot more, *any* of us who wants to change our Self-Talk can do it. Millions of people with overwhelming programs of negativity have done it—so if *you'd* like to change your Self-Talk and your programs, you can.

To show you how, I'll summarize some of what we've learned during thirty years of studying Self-Talk, and bring the process down to its three simplest steps. (These are three easy steps you'll have fun using, and they work incredibly well.) Here are the steps:

1. *Monitor* your own Self-Talk.

To do this, listen to *everything* you say when you talk to yourself now, or when you talk to anyone else. Listen not only to what you say out loud, but also to what you think. Listen to every message you give yourself at any time and in every circumstance.

If you were to keep a notebook and write down everything you say for the next week, you might be astonished at what you'd find when you read the transcript of your own Self-Talk.

2. *Edit* everything you say, and everything you think.

You were born with the incredible gift of the ability to make choices about what you say and what you think. (That is a *great* gift, and one you should use.) You have the understanding and strength within you to stop yourself the moment *before* you are about to say something negative—and in so doing, make another programming mistake.

Editing your own Self-Talk takes practice. Your old programs don't want you to succeed at this, but if you work at it and stay with it, you can do it.

In doing that, you won't automatically change the old programs you got along the way—only repetition of new, more positive, Self-Talk programs will do that—but when you start *editing* your Self-Talk, you'll stop yourself from getting any *more* of the wrong messages programmed in.

If you hear in your mind that you're about to say something negative (like the things on the list of negative self-talk), or something you would *never* want to program into your mental computer, *stop* it. *Change* it. Immediately replace it with something positive and healthy. Do this every time a negative program comes along, and watch how quickly you see the difference.

3. Listen to the right kind of Self-Talk.

The best way we've ever found to change our programs is by listening to professionally recorded Self-Talk.

We learned our old self-talk through *repetition*—by hearing it repeated again and again, often enough to create strong, lasting programs in our computer brains. Today, when people want to change their old programs—with new Self-

Talk—they do it in exactly the same way, by listening to specially worded Self-Talk CDs.

The new Self-Talk gives us exactly the kinds of programs we should have gotten in the *first* place—strong, positive, uplifting, and motivating. We have learned that when you listen to new Self-Talk now, for even a few minutes each day, you begin to replace the old programs that held you back, with positive new programs that move you forward in any area of your life that you choose to work on.

Along with getting the *right* programs, one of the reasons you should listen to Self-Talk is that every time you listen, you are reminded again of who you *really* are and what you can really do.

(Good times to listen to Self-Talk are first thing when you get up in the morning, while you're exercising, for a few minutes anytime during the day, just before an appointment or a business presentation, while you're riding in the car, and just before you go to bed at night. If you're an Arbonne consultant, or just want to be more successful in any way, you should listen to Self-Talk—even a few minutes of it—every day, or several times a week at a minimum.)

It would not be an overstatement to say that, along with using the other "gifts," the most important thing you can do *first* is to take the time to make sure you've got the right Self-Talk.*

Your old programs can be replaced, if you override them with new Self-Talk programs that are stronger. Fortunately, you can do that by listening.

* *You can obtain professionally recorded Self-Talk CDs online at www.selftalkstore.com.*

Put the Right Self-Talk Into Everything You Do

Anyone who wants to do this can, because that's the way the brain works. If you have old programs that are holding you back, you have to "input" better programs into your mental computer.

In my own life, I lost 58 pounds in less than 10 ½ weeks by listening to Self-Talk (in those days, on cassettes). That was more than twenty years ago! The weight never came back, and I've been listening to and using Self-Talk in virtually every area of my life ever since.

If you want to succeed in your business, get healthier or lose weight and keep it off, build your self-esteem, improve your relationships—whatever your objective—add the right, new Self-Talk to whatever you're doing now to reach your goal. And get rid of, once and for all, the programs that have been stopping you or holding you back.

Remember:

Change your Self-Talk and you change your programs. Change your programs and you change your life.

Chapter 8

The Gift of *Exceptional* Attitude

W hen you look for it, you can see your own attitude. You can see it the first thing in the morning when you wake up. You can see it in the mirror when you're getting ready for the day. You can see it at breakfast. You can see it at work, when you're with other people, or when you're by yourself. And you can especially see it when you're confronted with the challenges or the problems of the day.

If you were to study your attitude carefully, you would find that more than anything else, it is your *attitude*—at any given moment—that is *choosing* how well your day is working. And if you add all of those moments together (all of your days and weeks and months of attitude *moments*), you would find that more than anything around you, it is your *attitude* that has been choosing how well your *life* has been working.

You've probably noticed how that same thing is true of other people you've observed. I see it in everyone around me—even people I don't know. Here's just one example.

Early one morning I was standing at the departure gate at a busy airport, waiting to board my plane. The plane was late and the waiting area was packed. So while I was waiting, as I often do I studied what I could see of the "attitudes" of the people around me—their expressions, how they were dealing with the plane being late, what they were saying, and in general how they were handling their lives at that moment. It was as though I could almost see their *entire lives*—reflected in the attitudes they were displaying, even in just those few minutes.

There was little doubt which of the people in the waiting area with me were in *control* of their lives—and which of them were controlled *by* their lives.

On this occasion, I noticed one older, somewhat disheveled woman in particular, who was clearly in a bad mood, and she was taking her unhappiness out on everyone around her. When she finally turned to face my direction I couldn't help but smile when I saw the word "GRUMPY" printed in large, bold letters on the front of her sweater.

Your own attitude, at any moment, says a lot about you—like it was printed in bold letters on whatever you're wearing that day. And over time, it is your attitude, how you're "thinking," each day, that determines whether you're making your life work—or not. That makes the gift of having an *exceptional* attitude *vital* to your future.

What Does it Say on the Sign That You Wear?

Imagine a T-Shirt store that sold only "Attitude" T-Shirts. Imagine actually wearing a sign (emblazoned on your T-shirt) each day, that clearly stated your attitude that day. Here's just a sample of the attitude "signs" you could wear—if your attitude was not the best:

"GRUMPY"

"DON'T BOTHER ME—I'M BEING DEPRESSED"

"TODAY JUST ISN'T MY DAY"

"CASUALTY ZONE"

"WORRIED AND INEFFECTIVE"

"UNABLE TO COPE"

"GIVING UP AND GIVING IN"

If you don't want to live that way, with those kinds of "signs" on your T-shirt, you can do better. On the "up" side of signs that you could wear, your T-shirt could say something like this:

"LIFE IS GREAT!"

"TODAY IS MY DAY!"

"I'M SMILING BECAUSE I'M ME!"

**"I HAVE AN ATTITUDE . . .
AND IT'S POSITIVE!"**

"YOU CAN COUNT ON ME!"

"LIFE WORKS!"

**"IF YOU'RE BEING NEGATIVE,
I CAN'T HEAR YOU!"**

**"WANT TO GET BETTER?—
ASK ME HOW!"**

You can see why the gift of having an exceptional attitude is another of the special gifts that is practiced by thousands of Arbonne consultants every day. As I mentioned earlier, when you meet one of them, it's not just the glow from their complexion that you notice; it's that *other* glow, the one that comes from the inside—from their *attitude.*

(Not all Arbonne consultants started out with bright, winning attitudes, of course, but being a part of the Arbonne organization is like surrounding yourself with healthy, upbeat, positive attitudes—like being on an Olympic workout team whose category is "personal growth." At the heart of that growth, is attitude.)

You might, on any given day, have a good attitude, a bad attitude, or one that's just average—but you're busy, you're getting through the day, and stopping long enough to give yourself an attitude checkup isn't on your agenda. *It should be.* Giving yourself the right attitude affects everything you do.

Having an Exceptional Attitude Is Much More Than Wearing Rose-Colored Glasses

Although it's true that you can have a "good" attitude or a "bad" attitude, and that's how we usually think about it, your attitude goes far beyond that.

What "attitude" really means is the perspective from which you view your life. It's how you see yourself and other people, and how you view what's happening around you at any given moment.

Choosing your attitude is like having different filters you place in front of a pair of glasses that you wear. Only these filters don't just change what you see from regular to rosy; they have the power to change how everything looks—from bleak to bright; from uncertain to sure; from dull and lifeless to vibrant and alive; from being short-sighted to having unlimited vision.

Another way to see your attitude—and the role it plays in your life—is to recognize that we all have many personality traits. We have our *happy* self and our *unhappy* self, our *moody* self and our *vibrant, full-of-life* self, our *fearful* self and our *courageous* self, our *timid, limited* self and our *strong, unlimited* self, our *angry* self and our *loving, forgiving* self, our *doubtful* self and our *believing* self—and many more personality traits like those.

Some of these work for us, and some of them work against us. But one or more of them is always on stage with us. And which of your traits you bring to the stage at any moment, is up to you.

What You Have—From Here on Out— Is *You*, and Your *Attitude*

What you have to work with in your own life, from today onward, is *you*—and the *attitude* you decide you're going to bring with you.

That's it. It won't be luck or chance that gets you where you want to go next. It will be *you*, and it will be your attitude—the way you approach your life every day—that will make it work for you.

The "you" that you bring with you is made up of your talents, your skills and your abilities. But if you want to do something special with your life, you will have to also bring the right *perspective*—the right attitude. And you'll have to use it every day.

Why is "Attitude" so Important? Your *Attitude* is *Everything*

Your "attitude" is not some abstract facet of your personality. Your attitude, in reality, is the role you choose to play out in your life every day. It is made up of your feelings, your temperament, your thoughts, your opinions, your frame of mind, your point of view, how you feel, and how you look at everything you do. It is the identity you take on, each and

99

every day. Like the glasses that change your perspective, your attitude is the lens through which you see yourself and your life—and act it out.

In that context, your "attitude" goes far beyond something as simple as a "good" attitude or a "bad" attitude—brought on by the emotion of the moment, or the way you feel at the time. In this larger sense, your *attitude* is how you *choose* to approach the next moments of your life—every hour of the day.

Your Own *Attitude* Controls Virtually Everything About You

If your mind isn't right, your life won't be right. Along with using the right Self-Talk to change your programs, getting your mind right means getting your attitude right. And that's essential, because your attitude controls or influences virtually *everything* about you.

To give you some examples of the importance of creating an exceptional attitude, here are just a few of the things your own attitude affects or controls in your life every day:

Whether you believe in the best—or in the worst

How you feel mentally, and emotionally

How much stress you have

How you feel physically

What you eat and how much

How much energy you have

How positively or how negatively you see the moment

How you react to problems

How you deal with the people around you

How you communicate—in every word you say

How you see yourself

How other people see you

How you treat yourself

How other people treat you

How much self-confidence you have

Every choice or decision you make

How clearly you think

What you think about

Whether you think in terms of your limitations or in terms of possibilities

Whether you take action—or do nothing

Whether you will have an average day, or have an exceptional day

Those are just a few of the things your own attitude affects in your life right now. As you can see from just that short list, much of your life could be said to be based on "good attitude, good day—bad attitude, bad day." But the attitude you choose takes you far beyond that.

Virtually *everything* you experience, every day, is affected by your attitude. That includes everything from how you answer the telephone to what you say next, who you choose to go to lunch with, what you do, what you put off doing, how much you get done, and what you plan to do tomorrow.

The greatest and the smallest moments of your life are defined and created by your attitude—which influences virtually *everything* you think, say, or do. That makes your attitude incredibly important.

What If You Could *Immediately* Make Your Life Work Better—Just by Changing Your Attitude?

Think about that for a moment. What if, along with your personality, your talents, your dreams, and every great thing in front of you in your own life, right now—what if the *one* thing that could bring it all together and make it work was nothing more than your *attitude*?

If you spent the next 30 days, and then the next 60 days, and beyond—if you worked every day on making your own *attitude* incredibly "right"—you could do *anything*. With the right attitude, you could overcome any fear, defeat any problem, see the best in yourself, set any goal, keep yourself *up*, overcome the obstacles, and reach the goal.

If you chose to do that, it wouldn't be magic, nor would it be luck. It would be *you*—and it would be your *attitude*—that made it happen.

102

What Changing Your Attitude—to an *Exceptional* Attitude—Will Do For You

The right attitude can change everything. It can literally turn your day around—day after day—and thereby, your life.

An exceptional attitude changes your "vision," your picture of how you see yourself and everything in your life, right now. It builds your spirit. It unleashes your creativity and shows you what works—instead of what doesn't work. It gives life to your day. It changes dark to light.

This kind of attitude lets you feel good about yourself again. It surrounds you with the energy of belief. It pulls you out of "average" and reminds you, once again, of what you can do, instead of what you cannot.

Instead of showing you only the problem, an exceptional attitude reminds you of your purpose. Instead of allowing you to see yourself as "wanting" or "lacking," it reminds you of your worth. It calms your mind, and levels out your day. It puts value back into the little things you do, and shows you how important even the smallest things you do can be. And it puts *you* back in control of you.

When you decide to have an *exceptional* attitude, those are the kind of results you can expect. When you change your attitude, you change your "fate,"—what you thought was to be—what you imagined was your only path. The simple act of *choosing* to have an exceptional attitude, by itself, can immediately change your path and move you in a better, more positive direction.

Our Attitude is So Much a Part of Us
It's Easy to Ignore

In spite of how powerfully important our attitude is, it's often easy to ignore. That's because our attitude is *always* with us. So whatever our attitude is, we get used to it, and take it for granted. We say, *"That's just the way I am—and there's nothing I can do about it."* If our attitude is down, our old self-talk tells us, *"I'm just having a bad day."*

Our attitudes are like the air that surrounds us, an invisible aura we carry with us that's always just "there." And since it's always there, just a part of us, we can go through days or weeks without even thinking about it at all. In fact, most of us are generally unaware of our own attitudes, unless for some reason it's unusually great on one day, or unusually depressed or down on another.

And in between, we do little or nothing with this awesome gift of personal growth—a life-force so powerful it can literally reshape our day in an instant.

Your attitude is the single most powerful tool you have at your disposal. It can do more to change your day, each day, than any other talent, skill, gift, or tool that you have.

So if something as commonplace as simple attitude is that important, why do many few people spend so little time working at getting it right?

Getting Their *Bodies* in Shape
—but Ignoring Their *Minds*

As just one example, I know people who spend 30 or 40 minutes every morning jogging along the street in their neighborhood, pumping hand weights, and practicing breathing exercises, working to get themselves in great shape—while the whole time going over an endless list of problems at the office, or worrying about things that are going on in their lives.

And then those same people who are so determined to get their physical selves in healthy condition will shower, get dressed, jump in the car and head off to work—without taking a single *minute* to exercise something else which is just as important as their physical conditioning, and could be far *more* important for their day: their *mental* conditioning—their *attitude*!

(The reason for this is that we're used to looking at ourselves in the mirror, and assessing what kind of shape our bodies are in. We're less used to looking at ourselves in the mirror and assessing what kind of shape our *minds* are in.)

Other people may be aware of their attitude, and they know it's important, but they're too busy to take the time to make an adjustment. They just keep moving through each day, never taking a break from the routine and asking themselves if their attitude is as it should be. Is it the powerful ally it was designed to be? Or is their own attitude doing little more than simply reacting to the whims of the world and the attitudes of the other people around them?

And there is yet another group of people who simply don't have any idea how much influence their own attitude has in their everyday lives—nor do they have any idea that *they* alone are ultimately responsible for that attitude.

To Own Your *Life*, You First Have to Own Your *Attitude*

This is a case of wresting control of your life from the uncaring influence of the world around you. If you're not consciously managing your own attitude, then your attitude (like the "choices" you make that we talked about earlier) is being managed *for* you—by someone or something else—and that usually means by the people around you or by the environment you live in or work in.

Think how you feel when you have to be around people of a negative nature. Or people who are grumpy and unhappy with the world most of the time. Or people who are critical of you or others, or socially abusive. Their unhealthy attitudes imprint *their* negative energies onto *your* attitude. If you don't know how to protect your attitude when you're around them, you can go from *up* to *down*—in just *moments*.

Protect Your Attitude at All Times

If you're not aware of what's happening to your attitude when other people are inflicting their less-than-healthy attitudes on you, then you fail to protect yourself from the onslaught. Like being smitten with a virus of darkness, carried by those who don't have enough light in their lives, when you're around those people your own attitude darkens, your spirit lessens, and the day changes from bright and promising, to gray and cheerless.

Where did your bright cheerful attitude from only minutes earlier go? Because your attitude was *left unprotected*, it simply reacted to the negative energies coming in from someone around you and responded in kind—sending immediate chemical messages to your brain, shutting down the cheer and turning on the gloom.

As an example of this, something as simple as a ten-minute argument in the morning dumps enough toxic levels of chemicals into your brain, that it takes the next *eight* hours just to get back to normal, so that you are "yourself" once again. This means that if you allow yourself to get into an argument or an emotional confrontation, you're leaving your attitude entirely unprotected, and open to a *chemical* attack.

It's Not Just *People* that Affect Your Attitude—It Can Be *Anything*

It isn't just *other* people and *their* attitudes that can make you feel like that. It could be *anything* at all—getting caught in traffic, having a tough day at the office, being tired, learning some bad news, or waking up in the morning and finding that it's raining again. Anything around you, *if you let it*, can affect your attitude in a negative way.

The key words there are, of course, " . . . *if you let it.*" You can let anyone or anything get to you, bother you, change your mood, or affect your attitude. In fact, with your own negative self-talk, you can even do those things to *yourself!* (Which is why you should make *sure* your own Self-Talk is *always* the *right* kind.)

Knowing how easily your attitude can be influenced, often negatively, by outside input, or the wrong self-talk, it's clear that if you want to live up to your best, you have to make sure your own attitude is the best—not *sort of* best, but the *very* best—attitude you can create.

Four Key Steps to Getting and Keeping an Incredible Attitude

There are four important steps to building, protecting and maintaining your attitude.

1. **Awareness:**
    Always *"be aware"* of your attitude. All the time, every day.

    Right now, ask yourself, *"How is my attitude today?"* (How is your attitude right now?)

    When you look at yourself in the mirror in the morning, smile. Tell yourself it's going to be a good day: *"I feel great! I'm ready for the best, and I'm going to make today an incredible day!"* That's not only good Self-Talk; that's Self-Talk that sets up your attitude up for the day ahead.

    But don't just give yourself a morning attitude boost and let it go at that. During the day, think about your attitude. Practice dealing with every day in the most positive way. And keep your attitude "up." (That doesn't mean you ignore the problems of the day; that just means you choose to deal with them in a more positive way.)

2. **Ownership:**

Always *"own"* your own attitude. Never let anyone or anything around you, own or control your attitude for you.

No one has the right to determine your attitude for you. Your attitude is solely yours to create and yours to own. The question, then, is do you always own your own attitude? Or do you, at any time, allow someone else, or something that's going on in your life, to create your attitude for you?

It is your right to look in the mirror in the morning and say, *"What kind of attitude do I choose to have today?"* As to what kind of attitude you choose to have at any given time, remember that your answer may not be just a simple, "A good one."

You may, as an example, have a difficult meeting to attend, and you may have to put on the armor of strength, high energy, and a high-power personality. (You can put on a more relaxed attitude later.)

Or you may have to spend time counseling one of your group members, and your day may call for a lot of listening and a lot of understanding. So that's the attitude you would choose.

Or maybe you're at the beach, and for the moment you don't have a care in the world, and you want to keep it that way. So you *consciously* choose to have an attitude of serenity and peace of mind. (An attitude you can also choose to have at home, if you like.)

Whatever the case, you choose the attitude. Don't let someone or something *else* choose it for you.

3. Protection:

Always protect your attitude from anything that would diminish it in any way. Never allow anything around you to take your spirit from you.

No one has the right to take your spirit or your attitude from you. The world, being what it is, may try, but don't let it.

Never let anyone else *ever* pull you down. In your own mind, and in your own attitude, pull yourself back up. No matter what you face, keep your own counsel, and be true to yourself. Take charge of your own attitude. Never, ever, let anyone else control your attitude for you.

You can't avoid every negative person or every negative experience, but you can protect your attitude from being stolen from you. The solution to this is to immediately be aware of what's happening, and instantly use the right kind of Self-Talk to counteract the attitude theft:

I choose my own attitude, and nothing and no one can take it from me.

Right now, this moment, and for this entire day, I choose to have a great attitude. That's my attitude, and that's my choice!

I feel great! I'm in control of my attitude and I'm in control of my life. I feel great already . . . and I'm getting better by the moment!

Try *that* when someone pulls in front of you when you're

110

driving, or when your boss yells at you or when you were just about to get into an argument at home.

Another amazingly effective attitude technique is one I learned while teaching children to have a good attitude. I taught them to, when something went wrong, simply point at themselves, smile, and say the words, *"Happy Attitude!"*

I use this one a lot, especially when I'm driving in heavy traffic and some of the other drivers around me *clearly* are not working on their attitudes!

Go ahead. Try it for yourself, right now. Point at yourself and smile and say out loud, *"Happy Attitude!"* See what I mean? (It's a great technique to teach your kids—and something you may want to do yourself anytime you need to—when you're pretty sure no one's watching.)

4. Improvement:
   Always *"build"* your attitude, every day, in every posi-tive way.

As you can imagine, one of the best ways to build your attitude is by listening to Self-Talk. While you're listening, and the positive, new Self-Talk is sending repeated messages to your brain for permanent storage, those same messages are being heard consciously, by you, and they're very motivating and energizing. So it's almost impossible to have a "down" attitude when you're listening to "up" Self-Talk.

That kind of positive, uplifting Self-Talk, when listened to the first thing each morning, as an example, sets your attitude and your "tone" for the entire day. When you frequently start your day in that way, you begin to develop the habit of thinking in that new, more positive, confident mode—and the "negatives" from others or the problems of the day no longer control your attitude for you. You're literally *creating* the attitude that lifts up your day.

Your Personal Attitude Checklist

In addition to listening to the right Self-Talk to build your attitude each day, here is a checklist that will help. It's a checklist that you could use every day.

If you'd like to know how your attitude is now or at any time, or if you'd like to immediately help yourself boost your attitude, carefully read the questions on the list, think about your answers, and listen to what they're telling you.

1. How is your attitude right now? (Is it Poor, Fair, Average, Good, or Exceptional?)

2. On a scale of 1 to 10, how is your attitude usually? (Poor, Fair, Average, Good, or Exceptional?)

3. If there is one thing you would like to change about your attitude, what would it be?

4. If you write a list of the things that usually build your attitude "up," what would you write on your list?

5. If you were to write a list of the things in your life right now that bring your attitude "down," what would you write on your list?

6. How important do you think your own attitude is, in managing your *daily* life to its best?

7. How important do you think your own attitude is, to creating the best in your *future*?

8. Is there anything right now that is affecting your attitude in a negative way? If there is, what can you do to change that?

9. If you could do one thing to change your attitude for the better, most days, what would it be?

10. If you were to set one goal about your own attitude, for the next 30 days, what would it be?

You Are Your Attitude

I've often been confounded by the people who did not get this simple idea of changing their attitude for the better the first time they heard it. It makes sense that if almost everything we *do* in our lives is directed entirely by our attitude at the moment, then everything we do must be the result of the *attitude* we choose to have—at the *moment*.

It was the great twentieth-century psychologist, William James, who said, *"The greatest discovery of my generation is that a human being can alter his life by altering his attitudes of mind."*

William James was right. The attitude you choose to have, right now, or at any moment, will change how you look at everything around you. And those attitudes, whatever they are, will change your life.

What You *Expect* is What You *Get*

There is a truth of human behavior, which, not surprisingly, is borne out by the field of quantum physics, that suggests that what you *expect* most is what you will get. In other words, what you *believe most* about your own future is very likely what will happen—in your own future. Scientists are now telling us that you literally create or influence much of what happens to you by *expecting* it to happen.

In the field of behavioral psychology, we have also found this to be true. What you think about most, what you believe most, will determine what happens to you most. People who expect the best tend to get the best. At the same time, people who believe in the worst about themselves tend to get the worst possible results.

In the self-portrait of your own life, *"what you see is what you get."* If that's true, and it is, that we live out the pictures of ourselves we see the most, why would *anyone* want to paint a *life picture* that is less than the best?

So you might as well *go for it!* Expect the best. Always look for the positive. Visualize yourself achieving your goal. *Invite in the good—and the good will bring its friends.*

What is the "Sign" That You'll Wear Tomorrow?

Tomorrow morning, when you wake up and prepare for

your day, what message—what words about your own attitude—will you print on the sign that you will wear? Will it be *"Today just isn't my day?"* Or will it be *"Today is my day—and nothing can stop me now!"* (That would be a good T-shirt to wear, tomorrow. But more than that, that would be a good way to live your life.)

You can give yourself the gift of an exceptional attitude—an attitude that shows you the best and lets you know every day, no matter *what*, that you *can* do it and you know you can! And with that kind of attitude, wherever it is you're headed, you're going to have a wonderful time getting there!

Next, to make sure you know exactly what you want and where you're going, let's look at the gift that will show it to you. It is the gift of *finding your focus*.

Chapter 9

The Gift of Finding Your Focus

T his gift is the gift of finding exactly what you want, so your focus is clear, your energy is strong, and your chances of reaching your goals are high.

Your greatest energy is created by your clearest focus. When your focus is clear, you know what you want and where you're going, and that generates more energy in your life.

There's a huge thing that happens when you focus intensely on something that's important to you. You're actually, physically and chemically creating more energy within you. It's an incredibly positive process that you should use to your advantage.

It wouldn't make any sense to *not* know what you want, of course. But a surprising number of people *don't* know. And if you don't have a clear idea of what you really want, it's certain you'll never get it. When you don't know what you want, you also do a lot of wheel-spinning—driving hard but not really getting anywhere.

People work harder and less efficiently when they don't know what they want, so they use up a huge amount of energy trying to accomplish the *wrong* things. Because they don't know what they really want, they don't know yet what the *right* things are.

A Lot of Very Bright People Don't Really Know What They Want

While most people would agree that you have to know where you're going to get there, a lot of those people themselves don't know what they really want. It's like saying, "I understand that I need to know what I want; I just don't know what it *is*."

When I ask the question, "What do you really want?" in a live seminar, and give members of the audience the opportunity to share their answers with the group, many people have a hard time coming up with a clear answer. It's not just a few people who don't know the answer. A *lot* of very bright people don't really know what they want.

If someone were to ask you, right now, "What is your *focus*, what do you really want?" what would you say? Do you *know* what you want specifically, and so clearly that you can see it in your mind and describe it in detail?

To Get Where You Want to Go,
You Have to See the Picture Clearly

If you're talking to people around you in the everyday world, the most typical responses you'll get to the question are answers like "I want a good family and a good relationship," "I'd like to be happy, and fulfilled," "I'd like to be healthy and have a good career." Or they might say "I want to help other people," or "I want my kids to get a good education."

All of those are honorable objectives, of course, but with no more insight or depth of detail, they become little more than broad, undefined, general goals, hopes and wishes. They may be good pictures, but they are pictures without focus or detail.

The People Who Have Their Futures in *Focus*

On the other hand, a focused person would sound more like this: *"I know where I'm going, and I know why I'm going there. I know exactly what I want, and I know exactly what I need to do to reach every goal I've got!"*

Now imagine that same person going on to tell you their specific action plan for each goal, clearly describing in detail each step that needs to be taken along the way. (That isn't a person who is overconfident. That's a person who has *clarity* and strength of purpose.)

The "focus" we're talking about here isn't a general, overall purpose or direction in life, like having a good family or having a million dollars in the bank. The focus we're

118

discussing here is clarifying *every* important step you're creating in the weeks and months ahead of you. To know what you want and to create the best in your future, you have to have the clearest, most detailed picture possible—today—of where you want to be tomorrow.

Taking a Snapshot of the Future You're Creating

To see that picture clearly, let's imagine you're talking to three of your friends.

The first of your friends has no real goals, and isn't really sure what she wants out of life.

The second friend has *some* idea of her goals, but she still can't really see them all that clearly.

Your third friend, meanwhile, has spent a lot of time focusing on what she wants and where she's going, so she already has a clear picture of her goals, and her future, in her mind.

Now let's say you had a special camera that could take a picture of what each of your three friends "sees" in her mind when you ask her what her focus is—what she really wants.

As you ask the question of each of them, you aim your special camera at them and take a picture. When you see the picture appear on the view screen on your camera, you're able to see the exact picture each of them was seeing in their minds the moment you took the picture.

When you look at the first picture, the one you took of your first friend, the one with no *idea* what her real goals were, there is little to look at—just a lot of blurs with indistinct patches of something or other here or there. The picture

119

of her future is completely out of focus.

When you examine the picture of your second friend, the one who has "some" idea of the life she really wants—but she's not quite clear about it yet—you can see images on the screen, and some of them you can kind of make out, but even those are just not clearly focused.

In your third friend's picture—the one who knows exactly what she wants, and also knows *exactly* what she has to do to get there—you can see every single goal in crystal clear focus, full of color and detail.

Your "Picture of Life"

If those were the kind of pictures we put on the refrigerator door to help us visualize our futures, I doubt that you would suggest to your first two friends that they put their pictures on the refrigerator—except to remind themselves of what they're doing wrong—and that's not very positive motivation.

But the third snapshot, the one that's beautiful and bright and crystal-clear, is the kind of "picture of life" you'd like to make a giant poster of and hang on the wall. *That's a future! That* one is going to work!

With the two first snapshots, it's easy to see what's wrong—but it's also easy to see the solution. Their *futures*, like their pictures, are out of focus. And if the picture you see through the lens of a camera is out of focus, what do you do? You adjust the focus, and *keep* focusing it until the picture gets clear and sharp.

So the people who haven't found their focus, in almost every case, are people who haven't spent enough time looking through the lens at their own future and adjusting the focus until the picture becomes clear.

How Clear is *Your* Picture? What Do You See When You Look Through the Lens?

This is another of those important times to take a moment and think about it. Right now, what do you see when you look through that lens and focus on your own future? Are the images vague and indistinct, or can you clearly see each part of your own tomorrows? And if not, what can you do about it?

In your own life, your own success will depend on how much clarity you have in knowing what you want. Yet, if you don't know exactly what you want, and in precise detail—if you don't automatically *have* focus—how do you get it?

There Is No *"Instant Focus"*—You Have to Take the Time to Do This for Yourself

There is no instant focus button on the lens of life. When it comes to visualizing a clear picture of your own future, you have to work at it and readjust it and fine-tune it until the picture of your future comes alive.

With that in mind, then, when you hear the question, *"What do you really want?"* take the time to visualize your mental snapshot of your own future, or any part of it, and just describe what you see. If you can't see something, in one area or another, *clearly* enough, then focus. And *keep* focusing until the picture gets so clear that you can easily describe what you see in the picture of your future.

Creating Your Future in Advance

I'm not suggesting that we are beyond human and have the power to determine everything about our futures. But the truth is we have been given a power, a great and special gift, to create much or even *most* of that future for ourselves. All we have to do is use the gift.

Just like the rule of life says as we discussed in the previous chapter, *"You will become most, what you expect most,"* you and I, through the pictures we have of ourselves in our minds, write the scripts that the future will find us playing out.

This concept should immediately bring to mind the popular personal growth technique of "visualization,"and the various methods you can apply to put visualization into practice. Those techniques include everything from practicing pictured meditations, to going in to the car dealership and test-driving a new car months before you get it, to papering your mirror with pictures of the life you want—just like putting the snapshot of your future on your refrigerator door.

30 Questions About Your Future

What do you see when you look into your own future? What do you *want* to see? To help you find out, here are thirty questions I recommend you ask yourself frequently—to make sure you have a clear picture of the exact future you would like to create. Answer each one of the questions with a description of the picture you'd *most like to see*. When you answer, be as descriptive and as detailed as you can. (That's how you create focus.)

When you answer these 30 questions, you could go just a year or two years into your future, or even five years or more—any future date you'd like to look at. But for now, we're going to go to today's date, exactly *two* years from now.

What will the actual date be exactly two years from today? If you could go forward in time, two years into the future from this moment, *what would you most want to see?*

(You may want to take this "focusing quiz" with your mate, or with a friend, so you can answer the questions out loud and actually hear your responses. Or, if you're alone, answer them out loud to yourself, so you can hear your answers clearly and completely. But either way, spend some time with this exercise. What you see when you answer is more than important—it's your *future*. Make it a good one.)

30 Questions About Your Future *Two Years From Today:*

1. *What is your job, or what are you doing as your vocation?*

2. *Where do you spend your daily "work" time; that is, what is your physical environment? (Home, office, in your car, on the beach . . .)*

3. *Are you doing, for your work, exactly what you'd*

most like to be doing?

4. How many hours a day do you work?

5. How many days a week do you work?

6. How many days or weeks of vacation time, or off-time do you have each year?

7. How successful are you in your work?

8. How much do you earn each year (specifically)?

9. How much money do you have in the bank, or in investments (specifically)?

10. What debts do you owe, if any?

11. As a result of your work, are you reaching your longer-term objectives? (What are they?)

12. Is there anything still standing in the way of you reaching those objectives?

13. If there is, what are you doing about that—in the future picture of you?

14. What specifically do you do most to enhance your education or improve your mind?

15. In this future picture, who, if anyone, is working in your picture with you, and what do they do?

16. Who are your best friends?

17. Who, other than your family members, do you spend your time with most?

18. *What do you do most in your spare time?*

19. *What are some other activities you most like to participate in?*

20. *Describe your family in this picture.*

21. *How is your relationship with each of the members of your family?*

22. *How much of your time do you spend with your family?*

23. *In general, in this picture, what is the one thing you do that makes you the happiest?*

24. *In this picture, what, if anything, is something you do that makes you the least happy?*

25. *What has been your greatest accomplishment during the past two years?*

26. *Where do you live?*

27. *What kind of home do you live in? (Describe it in detail.)*

28. *What kind of car do you drive?*

29. *If you could change anything about your life in this picture, what would it be?*

30. *What are one or two goals you would like to accomplish in the following two years (after this picture)?*

If you had a personal life coach who talked with you frequently, say, every week or two, your coach would ask you many of those same questions. The difference would be that your coach would be asking you questions like those often enough for your answers to become so clear to you that you'd know *exactly* what you wanted to create.

Week after week, you'd be fine-tuning the focus of the lens through which you see your own future. In doing that, your picture would become clearer and clearer. Goal-setting would come easily to you, because you'd know *exactly* what you want. (Eventually, you'd know exactly what you needed to do—and every step to take.)

Your Best Possible Future Begins the *Moment* You See it *Clearly*

To do this, you have to spend time on yourself. But you're worth it, and it's one of the most valuable ways you'll ever spend your time. Talk about your future. Think about it. Tell yourself what you like and what you don't like. Share the picture of your future with trusted friends—those who are supportive—and each time you do, see the picture a little more clearly.

To do this well, you have to take the time to do it—*you have to devote this important time to yourself.* That's not self-centered—that's *essential*! Focus in life, for any of us, doesn't come by accident. Everyone, without exception, who has found their focus, has had to *take the time* to do it.

If you do the same thing, if you take the time, your pictures will become sharp and clear, and full of details. The moment you begin to see your future with that kind of bright, positive clarity is the moment you'll begin to create it.

What If You're Just Not Sure
What You Really Want?

A lot of people, even after they work on it for a short while, still aren't sure what their focus should be. Don't worry if you just can't see it yet. Finding what you want is a "skill," as well as an experience of exploration, and you have to practice. The more you work at it, the better you'll get.

I know people who haven't spent a solid hour of figuring out what they really wanted out of life since they sat down for twenty minutes with their guidance counselor in high school.

The more you sit down with yourself *now*, or with people you trust who believe in you, and keep asking yourself the same questions, the more the answers will come to you. Give it time; they'll come.

If You Really Want to Have an Incredible Future
—There's One More Thing You Have to Do

The final step in making sure you find your focus—and your fulfillment—is to *daydream*. (That's right. Do *exactly* what people told us to *stop* doing when we were kids.)

Daydream a *lot*. Every day. Daydream any chance you get—like on the way to work, or while you're relaxing in the bath, or just before you go to sleep at night, or anytime you have a few minutes with your own thoughts. Go for it! Dream! Visualize that you can have anything you can imagine. Have the time of your life. (You should. When you're daydreaming about your future, you're *creating* the time of your life.)

And don't worry about overdoing it. Just keep dreaming. Dreams—the kind of dreams you dream when you're awake—have a way of turning into goals, and then into plans, and then into action. *Daytime* dreams, visited often, have a way of coming true.

Ask yourself the question, ***"Who am I really, and what do I really want?"*** Write it on a card and carry it with you. Ask the question over and over—*Who am I really, and what do I want?* You might surprise yourself when, soon after you've begun doing that, you start to get some answers. And then, one day, out of nowhere, the answer jumps out at you, and you realize, *"That's who I am, and that's what I want!"* After that, you may find that actually *getting there* is the easy part.

Chapter 10

The Gift of Setting Great Goals

O nce you begin finding your focus in each area of your future, you'll continue to fine-tune it. But as *soon* as you see the first pictures clearly, it's time to take the next step. It's time to set some clear, simple goals.

The gift of setting goals is one of the most exciting of all of the gifts—and one of the most immediately *helpful* tools for personal growth, and actually making every day count. Learning how to set goals in the right way is a gift you'll have fun using from the first day you start.

Even though almost everyone would tell you that setting goals is one of the most *essential* steps for business success or personal growth, *less than 3%* of the people we meet *actually set goals for themselves* in any organized way. Only two or three people out of a hundred even write them down. They know goals are important, but they're too busy to spend any time with them—or they don't yet know how helpful setting the right goals can be.

Or, worse yet, old "negative" programs from their past cause them to see goals as *obligations*, or *responsibilities*, "something hanging over their head." That picture of goals is completely inaccurate, of course. That would be like avoiding looking at the map while you're driving on your vacation, because you think getting somewhere is something to avoid.

That's too bad. Without goals, we pretty much live life by chance. On the other hand, *with* good, simple, direct goals, the kind we write out, we change the odds—we know where we're going, and we change "chance" to "choice"—*our* choice.

But, since it's vital to set clear, well-defined goals if you want to get anywhere, the solution is in making setting goals so easy that you do it frequently, and look forward to it.

I'm going to share with you a way to make setting goals so easy to do that you can have a complete goal plan down on paper in just a few minutes. The easier it is, the more you do it, and soon it becomes exciting, because you start to see the results.

The Most Important Goals are Short-Term Goals—and They Must be Written Down

The most important goals are *daily*, *weekly*, and *monthly* goals (or anything less than a year away). You should set long-term goals, of course, but it's the short-term goals that actually get you there. They are the goals that make things happen, and move you toward the bigger, lifetime goals.

But these all-important daily, weekly and monthly goals *have to* be written out. (The moment you write a goal down, along with a simple plan to reach it, the chances of reaching that goal jump from about *five* percent to *seventy* or *eighty* percent!)

When you take the simple step of actually writing out your goals in the right way (instead of living your life each day following a shadowy road map to uncertainty, not knowing what you should do next), you're literally drawing a new map for yourself.

Instead of having no clear road map to follow, you can see precisely where you want to go, and what you should do next, each step of the way. Without goals, and clear steps to follow, you either don't know where you really want to go in the first place, or you easily get off course—sidetracked by the distractions of everyday living.

So when you don't have your next steps clearly laid out, you're held captive by the whims of everything that's going on around you. Things that aren't nearly as important as your goals demand your attention and take up your time—the precious few hours you have each day to stay on track and make a difference in your life.

The Choices You Make Are Governed By the Goals You Set—or by The Goals You *Don't* Set

When you're not in control of your own life—your own day, each day—someone or something *else* is in control of the

131

direction of your life.

If you don't have crystal-clear goals to keep you on track, all the dozens of big and small choices in your life each day are made by the chance encounter with the incidental trivia of daily life. So instead of *you* consciously making choices that do *you* the most good, the rest of the world around you is making your choices for you. Choices that may have *nothing at all* to do with you or your goals—or with what *you* wanted in the first place.

As we discussed in the earlier chapter on making choices, one of the most important keys to taking control of your own life is to take back control of your daily *choices* from the accidental circumstances around you. When you set clearly-defined goals, and stay mindful of them (not just occasionally, but every day), you do yourself a big favor. You put *yourself* back in control of your life. And your own life suddenly gets exciting and stimulating because *you're* in charge of it!

Six Easy Steps to Setting Great Goals

I have a positive "challenge" for you that will help you set good goals for years to come. I'd like you to follow these six simple goal steps for the next 90 days. (They're the same steps I follow with my own goals.) Whatever methods you may have used for setting your own goals up to now, try these steps for three months, and watch what happens.

Step 1. *The Goal*

Write down each of your goals. No matter how small or how big, *write each of them down.*

A goal that is not written down (or typed out on your computer) is not a goal. Until a goal is written out or printed out where you can read it and review it, it's merely a wish, a want, a hope, or a dream—but it's not a goal. At least not one you can see clearly, with the action steps that will bring it to life.

Now, when you write the goal, always start by writing the words, "My Goal is: *to* . . . and then complete the sentence:

"My Goal is: *to make a minimum of four business presentations a week.*"

"My Goal is: *to weigh 130 healthy pounds.*"

"My Goal is: *to read at least one positive book every month.*"

"My Goal is: *to get up 30 minutes earlier each morning.*"

"My Goal is: *to sing in the choir at church.*"

"My Goal is: *to earn $8,500.00 a month.*"

When you use the technique of writing all of your goals in that way, you'll find all of your goals easier to *define*, and *simple* to write.

Step 2. *The Date*
Date each goal with a *specific* date—*day, month,* and *year*.

Write down the *exact* date you intend to either *begin* the goal, or *complete* the goal. As an example, for the goal "My Goal is: *to become a better listener*" you would state the date you're going to start the goal, and start listening better. (That's a work in progress.) For the goal, "My Goal is: *to buy our new house,*" you would write in the date you're going to sign the papers.

Don't worry about "setting yourself up for failure" by writing in a specific date. You'll be reviewing your goal plans often. If you have to change the date, change it. Update it. (That's what *all* successful goal-setters do.) But you have to start with a specific date. If you don't, it's *not* a serious goal—or you doubt yourself and you're afraid to commit. But if it's a goal that you want to achieve, you have to commit.

Step 3. *The Obstacles*
Write out a simple list of obstacles to reaching your goal.

Write out a short list of one, two, or three obstacles you can see that could stand in the way of you reaching the goal you've just written down.

This step is key. If you don't write down the obstacles that could be in the way of reaching your goal, you won't know what action steps to take to overcome them.

This is the goal step that many goal-setting methods in the past have overlooked. But you can't afford to overlook it. Once you've figured out the goal and written it down, you *have* to know what stands in your way of reaching it.

Step 4. *The Action Steps*
After each "obstacle" you identify, write down the action steps you're going to take to overcome the obstacle.

Here's an example. Let's say you have a goal to earn a trip to Hawaii. So you write out the goal in its simplest words:

"My Goal is: *to earn the trip to Hawaii.*"

Next, you date the goal. In this case it would be the date by which you have to qualify to earn the trip.

Then, for Step 3, you write out any obstacles that could stand in the way of you earning your trip:

1. *I have to create more sales.*
2. *I have to sign up at least two new people in my business to earn the trip.*
3. *I haven't organized my schedule, and that's getting in my way.*

Now write a simple list of "*action steps*" that will tell you what to do about each of the obstacles you've just listed. You might write something like this:

Obstacle: I have to create more sales.
Action step: Call each of my clients and prospects and set up a time to get together. When I'm there, make sure I ask for the order and close the sale.

135

Obstacle: I have to sign up at least two new people in my business to earn the trip.

Action step: Make five new presentations by _____ (date).

Obstacle: I haven't organized my schedule, and that's getting in my way.

Action step: (For this one we'll say you've identified several action steps you decide to take.)

1. Organize my schedule.
2. Return all of my phone calls by noon each day.
3. Write e-mails between 8 and 9 AM.
4. Identify my time-wasters—anything I'm doing when I'm working that shouldn't be there—and stop doing those things.

(If following simple steps like those seems in any way like something that's difficult to do, it won't seem that way when you're sitting on a beach in Hawaii, and thinking about the people back home working in their offices from 9 to 5, or stuck in traffic on their way to work.)

Step 5. *The Review*
Review your "goal plan" at least once a week.

Reading through your goal plan only takes a few minutes. Write out the *goals*, the *dates*, the *obstacles*, and *the action steps*; print them out (if you're using a computer), and read your goal plan over carefully at *least* once a week. If you really want to give *life* to your goals, read it more often than that. Preferably once a day, first thing every morning, so that each day you'll be reminded of your goals, and you'll be more motivated to take the specific action steps you need to take to work on them.

Step 6. *The Reward*
Reward Yourself For Each Accomplishment Along the Way.

This step is as important as any of the previous steps to reaching your goals. When you reach a goal, or even any important step along the way, *acknowledge* it. Appreciate it. Congratulate yourself. Let yourself know what you've done!

When I'm working on a goal, no matter how big or small the goal might seem, I always set my rewards in advance. And it always works. It could be an afternoon off to see a movie because I finished writing a difficult chapter in a book. It could be just some time off to go horseback riding because I reached a benchmark on a project I was working on. Or it could be a special vacation with my family because I got a book finished or completed a speaking tour.

But in each case, set the reward—in advance. It can be anything that fits the accomplishment.

A woman told me recently she had finally gone to lunch with three of her best friends, something she hadn't done in too long a time. But she took the time off and did it, without guilt, because it was a reward she had decided on in *advance* for reaching her goal of changing her daily schedule and getting more organized. When she reached her goal, she called her friends and invited them to lunch.

137

The reason for the importance of these major and minor rewards is that the rewards we give ourselves are our "report card." We don't have a teacher, like we did at school, who gives us a gold star—so now, we have to do that for ourselves.

The rewards and the gold stars you agree to give yourself in advance for your own accomplishments on the way to your goals aren't just a way to make you feel better for a day. Those little and big rewards tell you that you *did* it. You're someone who succeeds, and you *know* it.

When you do that, you begin to create a "pattern of successes"—which in turn creates a picture of you as an achiever. And that's exactly the picture you're working to create.

Those few short steps to a more effective way of setting goals for yourself may be simple and easy enough to do. But the results of following those steps will have an effect on what happens in the next days and months—and *years*—of your life. And the only requirement is that you use them.*

What If You Could See the Next Five Years of Your Life—in *Advance?*

Would you like to see your future? (Remember, if you can see it, you can create it.) Let's take a look at it.

* *To set your goals online, and receive a personalized printout of your weekly goal plan and support from Dr. Helmstetter each week via e-mail, go to www.goals-on-line.com.*

To help you do this, we're going to use a video camera this time, so we can see more of the picture and see your life in action.

Let's say that you have in front of you right now two different videos of your life, each showing you in your future, five years from now. Each video is about 20 minutes long.

The first video is the one that is taken of you after *not* setting real goals for your next five years. In this first video of you, because you're a good person, you've done your best, but you've lived your life with no special, goal-driven direction—because you haven't taken the time to write out your goals or read them daily.

Now you watch the video of you and your life, seeing yourself in your own future on the television screen—and you *hope* to see that your life, five years from now—*without* goals—is working the way you'd like it to.

Your Life *Without* Clearly-Written Goals

As you watch the video of your future without goals, you see everything. In the short 20 minutes that it takes the video to play out, you learn what kind of job you will have; you discover what kind of home you'll live in; you see the car you'll drive then, and you even see some clips of you, talking to the camera—talking about your job, your income, and the life you're living.

I can't say for you what your life would look like in five years *if you set no goals*, or if you set goals but didn't take them seriously. That is a video of your future only you can imagine for yourself.

Your Life *With* Goals

But then, when the first video has finished playing, you put the second video in the player. This video shows the life you will be living if you *do* it—if you use the gifts of personal growth, *set every good goal you can set*, and work to reach them—for just five short years.

I have no doubt that this second, goal-directed picture of your future would be vastly different from the first video taken of your next five years where you *didn't* use the gifts or set the right goals.

In this short, 20-minute picture of your life five years from now, you would see the you who had chosen to set the goals that would change your life. In this video, you see a person who worked at their goals, found a lot of support, set their sights higher, made the choice to live out their dreams to the fullest, and decided to take control of their life, believe in themselves, and reach every goal they set—and it's *you*!

Which of those two videos of your life would you choose? The question almost answers itself, of course; all of us would choose the life that *works*—and that would be the life with *clearly written goals*.

If You Could Live the *Next* Five Years *Over* Again —What Would You Do *Differently* This Time?

We've heard people say, *"If I could live the last five years of my life over again, there are a lot of things I would do differently."*

But what if, somehow, you could live the *next* five years of

140

your life differently? What if you decided to get it right, set the right goals, have a clear picture of where you're going, use all the right tools, and made the choice to do it now, in advance?

If you do that, there's no telling what you could do! There's no telling what a picture of twenty minutes of your life could look like, just five years from now. Or three years. Or two years. Or even a year from now.

That's what setting the right goals, following the right steps, and using the "gifts" can do.

Of course, when you do that, it will be *you* who did it. The tools, and the gifts, and the goals will help. But it will ultimately be your choice to *do it* that gets you there.

More Programs of the Positive Kind

When you're setting goals, writing them out, and reviewing them regularly, you're *repeatedly* telling your subconscious mind, *"This is what I want. Now go to work on it. Help me get it."* By setting goals in this way, you're literally giving your computer brain positive, new directions (programs) to follow!

When you tell your subconscious mind, repeatedly, exactly what you want, it has no choice. It will do everything in its power, which is huge, to help you get it. Now *you're* the director of the movie you're filming of your own future.

So follow the steps. Write out your goals, and then read and review them every week—or every day if you can. You'll be amazed at how, as if by some kind of magic, your goals suddenly begin to materialize, out of nowhere, and the real story of your future begins.

By setting clear goals and following the action steps, you're about to be able to reach any goal you set. The next gift will help you make sure you've got the *time* you need to do that.

Chapter 11

The Gift of Taking Control of Your Time and Your Life

I magine how much we could accomplish in a year if we were given an extra *week*—every month of the year. We could get a lot more done and still have time left over for ourselves. What a wonderful gift that would be!

But life, for most people, isn't that generous. Just listening to our own self-talk on the subject of getting time under control is revealing. How often we hear ourselves saying things like, *"I never have enough time," "I don't know where the time went,"* or, *"There just aren't enough hours in the day!"*

Living On Island Time

While we might really care about getting things done and making the most of each day, we secretly wish we had the luxury of living on "island time" and not having to worry about things like clocks and schedules. (Tourists in the Virgin Islands are often told about the "island wrist watch." It's a woven bracelet or simple metal band, but there's no clock face on the island wrist watch. When you want to know what time it is, you simply look at the bracelet. If you can see it, it's daytime. If you can't see it, it's night.)

The solution to getting more free time, or extra time, or even island time, is in how you *use* the time that you have. It is almost a cliche that the people who are the busiest and get the most done, seem to have more *extra* time for themselves.

As one of the most important gifts you'll ever have, it makes sense to take the time to *actively* control your time. For a lot of people, that's not only easier said than done, it's also something that *never* gets done. (They don't have the time to take the time to do something about not having enough time.)

This is one gift that life-changers spend time working on. If you want to create a better future for yourself and your family, it makes sense that you would learn, as fast as possible, how to have more hours in a day and how to be more efficient with the limited time you have.

If You Want to Get in Control of Your *Life*, You Have to First Take Control of Your *Day*

There are many people who try to get in control of their lives—without first getting in control of their *days*. The end result of any goal always starts with its first step. That's also true of changing your life for the better.

Changing your life is a lofty goal, a goal that is sometimes hard to picture clearly. But knowing what you're going to get done in one hour, or in the next five minutes—that's something any of us can understand. And that's where changing your life for the better has to start—in your moments and hours. In what you do next, every day.

Ask yourself the question, *"Am I in control of my day, or is my day in control of me?"*

For most people, the answer is "some of both." That is, you probably feel you have *some* control over each day, but at the same time, you may often feel that too much of your day is *not* in your control. And since it's what you do with the time you spend going through each day that ultimately determines what you do with your weeks and months, it becomes clear that how you manage your time each single day is vitally important to your future.

The important choices you make about controlling your time each day should never be left up to your invisible, unconscious choices. They should be *conscious* choices—the kind of choices you think about, and about which you make clear, conscious decisions.

Unless you *consciously* think about putting each hour to the best use each day, the day goes on—all by itself—without your direction. It's like taking your hands off the steering

145

wheel and letting the car drive itself. Only in this case the car is your life. It's no wonder we meet so many people who are always driving off in the wrong direction—and wondering why they're not getting anywhere!

The Gift of Time

We are reminded now and then that time is precious and, along with our health, the most important thing we'll ever have. And we were told to manage it carefully—but with the demands of daily life pressing down on us, it's advice that is easy to forget. We tell ourselves, "I'll get in control of my time some other time. As soon as I have time. Right now I'm busy."

The problem is that we *get used to* life's demands getting in the way of us getting in control—we believe *that's the way life is.* We become convinced that we just have to learn to live with it. When we have jobs, and families, and obligations, and responsibilities, and bills to pay, we start to think, *"My time is not my own. It's not in my control."* And we think that and hear that often enough that it becomes a programmed "truth"—even though it's not true at all.

You May Have More Control Over Your Time Than You Know

The real truth is that you may have more control over your time, and what you do with it, than you've convinced yourself you have. (It just doesn't seem like it when you're late for work, the phone is ringing, you forgot to put gas in the car, it's raining, you just spilled coffee on your blouse, and one of the kids is yelling that the gerbil got out.) There are times when you just have to take a deep breath and let things pass. But the difference between living your life by taking a lot of deep breaths or living your life by design, is just that: living your life by *design. Your* design.

The fortunate thing about this is that time is a resource that virtually anyone can conquer and manage. Proof of this is that some of the most time-challenged, disorganized people I have ever known, have transformed themselves into on-top, in-control "directors" of their own lives. And they did it by first making the *choice* to get in control, and then following some basic, simple steps that would get them there.

The reason this is important to your own personal growth is that, without exception, women and men who are not in control of their time and their days almost never reach their goals or become truly fulfilled in their lives. The women who win, the men who excel, all have this one trait in common: they learn to "actively" control their time.

Four Steps to Actively Controlling Your Time

The bigger your goal, the simpler the steps to getting there have to be. If you'd like to have more time—free time, productive time, personal time, or just extra time—there are four steps you can take now to help you get it. (You can study half a dozen in-depth courses in time management, and the best of them always get down to a few very simple steps.)

Here are the key steps I've identified to *actively* control your time.

1. Practice *"Active" Time Control.* Be aware of what you do with your time, every hour of the day.

We only find *true* "freedom" when we exercise our choice to control our own space—our own environment—at least as much as we're able to. If we don't take control of our own lives, the world around us controls it for us. "Time," the hours we have in a day, is part of that.

To use this simple step of *actively* controlling your time, there is a tool you can use, and it works beautifully!

Each morning, after you've woken up—when you're in the shower, or getting ready for the day—ask yourself these questions:

"How will I actively control my time today? What will I do with my time today, and how will I use it in the best possible way?"

And then answer the questions. When you ask yourself the questions, and give yourself the answers, you set your day up differently. You let yourself know that your time today is important to you. Right now, today. And you've just made the choice to make the most of it.

Then, at night, ask yourself:

"What did I do with my time today?"

The reason to keep asking yourself these questions is to practice *"active"* time control by developing an active awareness of how you're spending your time each day. The more aware of your time you are, the more wisely you'll spend it—*especially* if, at the same time, you're working on reaching your goals, and reviewing them each day.

2. Set aside the time to plan your time.

Is where your time goes, up to you? Do you know what you're going to do tomorrow? Or each day this week?

When you're practicing "active" time control, along with increasing your awareness of how you spend your time, you should also keep a daily and weekly schedule—and do your very best to stick to it. You may already do that; all successful business people do.

The important thing with this step is that you actually set aside the time to do it. Make this an *active* time-control habit, not a passive, now-and-then activity. In less than five or ten focused minutes, you can plan an entire day—and *save* many minutes, or even hours—just by being more organized and knowing what you're going to do next.

If you take the time to plan your time each day and each week, you won't have to keep asking yourself where all the time goes. You'll *know* where it goes. And it will be your choice.

3. Each day, do what's important—and *actively* avoid what is not.

The key here again is the word "actively." If you want to reach your goals, and have true freedom in your life, you will have to *choose* to spend your time each day in the most

149

intelligent way. You have to control your time; you have to use your time *well*.

That doesn't mean you can't relax, take time off, stop and have a latte on the way to work, visit with a friend on your lunch hour, work a crossword puzzle, or go shopping for something you don't really need, because, at the moment, that's what *you* need to do. Those things, and many more like them, take up our time, and in many cases, it's time well spent. Maybe.

But there are also things that most of us find easy to agree to do, simply out of habit, which are *not* time well spent. Things like talking too long to the wrong "friend" on the phone, taking on too many parenting activities at your kids' school, putting extra time in at work—when you could be and should be doing something else, staying up too late watching a movie on television because you wanted to see the ending—and then falling asleep before the ending anyway, getting the food ready for a dinner party you didn't want to host in the first place, or just getting too busy to take any *real* time for yourself.

What you do with your time is up to you, of course. But *you* have to decide what's important to you, in the time you have, each day, to make your life work—not just *well*, but *very* well.

Above all, you have to take the time to make the time to make your life work the way you'd like it to. (If you'd like to do that, but haven't conquered this one yet, set a goal. Write it out. Give yourself the next 30 days to work on actively controlling your time, and at the end of 30 days give yourself a progress report.)

4. Add *days* of extra time to your month—every month.

I mentioned earlier that it might seem unattainable to have a free *extra week* of time every month. But if you'd like to have even a few extra days each month, you can.

I'll give you an example. Some years ago, I had made the decision to write a complete library of the best kind of Self-Talk—the words and phrases of positive Self-Talk that I knew would help people improve their lives, if they had the right Self-Talk to listen to every day.

But to write my library of Self-Talk, I knew it would take months of time. At the time, I was busy in every area of my life. I was raising a family, working more than full-time in my consulting business, and, at the same time, working on the outline of a book. My time was fully committed already; I had no spare time left over to dedicate to writing and creating the library of Self-Talk I wanted to write.

What I chose to do next changed my life. I decided to get up a half-hour earlier every morning, and spend that extra half-hour each day writing the Self-Talk. Instead of staying up to watch the late-night news on television, I decided to miss the news, and get up a little earlier each day.

In two or three weeks, I had figured it out. Instead of getting up at 7:00 AM, I could start writing at 6:00 AM. And then, because I had adjusted to the new hour, I moved my alarm clock forward another half hour, to 5:30 AM. It took a while, but I ended up waking up before the 5:30 alarm on my clock would sound. I would wake up, get up, make a cup of tea, and start writing. The result was that in the next few months of doing that, I wrote the Self-Talk library entirely on

151

free time—extra time—time when I would have otherwise been *sleeping*.

Sometime later I sat down with a calculator and figured it out. The result of just getting up an hour, or an hour-and-a-half, earlier, each morning gave me as much as an extra *forty-hour week—free—every month*.

You may not choose to get up at 5:30 every morning, but many very successful people use the technique of adding even a half an hour to their day—and many of them credit much of their success to that extra time they've added to their life.

If you use just *one* or *two* of those ideas for getting in control of your time and your life, you'll do better. If you put all *four* of those tools into practice, you will very likely have time to spare.

Now, to make sure you get started and stay with it, let's look at a gift that will put you into action, and keep you there.

Chapter 12

The Gift of Putting Yourself Into Action

Y|ou can't have success without taking action. That makes this gift pretty important. (Especially if you ever find yourself *not* taking action when you *should*.)

When you know it's time to get active, but you put it off, it will help if you know *why* you're not jumping in with both feet and getting it done. If you know what's stopping you, you'll know what to do about it.

There are five primary reasons people don't take action. When you know the reasons and what to do about each of them, you will find it easier to put yourself into action anytime you need to.

1. We don't take action if . . .
We don't really know what to do.

You can't take sensible action if you don't know what to do next. If you're unsure of yourself, or if you don't have a clear idea how to solve the problem or proceed, chances are you'll slow down—or stop.

Have you ever found yourself knowing that you're at a standstill in something you should be doing, but you just can't seem to get *active*? If the problem that's stopping you is that you're not sure what to do next, or how to *fix* the problem that's getting in your way, here's something you can do, immediately, that can help.

Who's Working on the Problem?

If things aren't moving forward, or if something is wrong, and you're not sure what to do next, ask yourself the question, *"Who's working on the problem?"* It's amazing how quickly this one question can get you pointed in the right direction.

Sales are down and you don't know why.
Who's working on the problem?

You're having trouble communicating with someone in your group, and it's slowing things down.
Who's working on the problem?

You're in a personal slump, and you can't seem to get back into action.
Who's working on the problem?

Your schedule has gotten so busy you're spending more time getting less done.
Who's working on the problem?

What's interesting is that almost every time you have to ask the question *"Who's working on the problem?"* the answer is usually, *"No one."* That is, no one is focusing on the problem 100% and coming up with the answer.

And if no one is working on the problem, then you have the first step to finding the solution to the problem. Because the moment you focus your attention on fixing the problem, instead of just letting it stand there in your way, you're one step closer to solving it.

There's No Problem that Can't be Solved— If Someone is *Working* on the Problem

The solution you come to may not be the perfect solution, or you may have to accept a partial solution of working *around* the problem instead of solving it entirely. But at least you'll be back in action and moving forward again.

Think of one thing right now, in your business or in your personal life, that may be keeping you from being *completely active*. Once you have a picture of it in your mind, ask yourself the question, *"Who's working on the problem?"*

Just spending time worrying about a problem or fretting over it is not "working on it." Giving it full attention and focusing on finding the solution is working on it. Part of doing that may be talking to people who've been there themselves and know the answer already. Or the solution may lie in just talking the problem through with someone to help you clarify what the *real* problem might be.

You may be surprised to see how quickly the solution appears once you identify the problem clearly, make a list of possible solutions, and actively work at solving it.

Some problems fix themselves. Most problems don't. They just stay there and, if we do nothing to solve them, they usually get worse. Yet, when you study the problem, figure it out so you see the *real* problem clearly, and then get the help or find the direction you need to fix it, you find that almost *no* problem is unfixable.

The solution starts with asking the question, *"Who's working on the problem?"*

2. We don't take action if . . .
We perceive the task as being too "difficult."

Some people put off doing things they perceive as being "difficult" to do. So instead of getting active, and getting the job done, they put it off. Their reasoning is, "This sounds difficult to me, so I'll do it later." (Even though it will *not* get *easier* later.) I know all of us have felt that way at one time or another.

What Does "Difficult" Really Mean?

I might think learning to ride a horse well is difficult. I might think raising kids in today's world is difficult. I might think that working at my hobbies of making stained glass windows or reading books on quantum physics is difficult. I might think that exercising or working out is difficult, or being on tour and traveling across the country for weeks to speak, or writing a book, is difficult.

Yet, at the same time, I *love* riding horses, raising kids, creating things from stained glass, reading, working out, traveling, speaking, and writing. So, then, why should those things be called "difficult?" Is it because they require effort? Because they take time? Because I have to work at doing them well?

I've studied the idea of what "difficult" is and what "difficult" is not, and I've come to some conclusions:

"Difficult" is twenty-one courageous settlers enduring four months traversing the Atlantic ocean to found the settlement of Jamestown, in Virginia, across three thousand miles of ocean in a "ship" that was no bigger than a small school bus.

"Difficult" is spending two decades making it possible to safely breathe in space, and then traveling from the Earth to the moon, so Neil Armstrong could stand on the first body of land outside of Earth and say the words, *"That's one small step for man, one giant leap for mankind."*

"Difficult" is Helen Keller, completely devoid of normal outside input, without sight or hearing and with no contact with the outside world other than "touch," becoming one of the most aware, positive and preeminent spokeswomen of the twentieth century for personal growth.

"Difficult" is the kids who compete in the Special Olympics and work their hearts out, in wheelchairs or on crutches, with little more than the encouragement and the cheers of their families and their supporters—just trying to stay in the race.

So when I hear the word "difficult," I think about it differently.

Difficult is *not* having to make a few more phone calls, meeting the sales quota at the end of the month, learning to be more outgoing, getting good at product presentations, or teaching someone new how to be successful.

When you are stopped by a problem, something that stops you from taking action, try seeing it as nothing more than the next grateful step you get to take to reach the goal.

In that way of thinking, making phone calls is not difficult. Neither is getting up a little earlier, emptying the e-mail box, or making a presentation to a group of friends. Things like that stop being difficult and become *"taking action."*

3. We don't take action if . . .
We haven't made the firm <u>commitment</u> to take the action we need to take.

The key to taking action is commitment—making the conscious *decision* to do it, and then standing by your decision. So if you're not taking action when you know you should, ask yourself what commitment you made to take the action. Did you make a clear, conscious decision to do it? Did you agree wholeheartedly with your decision?

Be Willing to Commit

Making commitments, big or small, and living up to them is one of the cornerstones of building positive character and personal growth. Children, as an example, who are taught the value of making good decisions, and committing to those decisions, are learning a tool that will help them excel in anything they do for the rest of their lives.

As adults, working on the lifelong quest of personal growth, the commitments we make give us the opportunity to practice, daily, living up to our best. So when we need to put ourselves into action when there's something we want to accomplish, our commitment to take action has to be greater than the reasons we have to put it off.

If you're putting off doing something you know needs to get done, ask yourself, *"What is my commitment to doing this?"* If, on a scale of 1 to 10, your commitment is anything less than a 10, then it's time to reevaluate your commitment. It could be that the task is *not* something that's as important to you as you thought it was.

If, on the other hand, taking the action is important to you, as a part of your plan for reaching one of your goals, then make the choice and recommit. And when you recommit, make it a *10*.

4. We don't take action if . . .
It's something we really didn't want to do in the first place.

I've often suspected that more garages get straightened up and cleaned out during the first two weeks in April than at any other time of the year—and not because it's time for spring cleaning. It's because for a lot of people, early April is *tax* time. Time to do the taxes: something almost *nobody* loves to do. So it's something that's easy to put off.

To justify putting things off, we find *other* things we have promised ourselves we'd do, and we do those things instead. So by the end of the weekend, the garage is spotless, but the taxes haven't been touched.

Some things, like getting that paperwork done, are things we have to do, and we know it. But there are other things we try to take action on, but don't quite have the zest for, because they are things we didn't really want to do to begin with.

Our "Procrastination" Shows Us the Things We Didn't Want to Do in the First Place

I recommend that you actually write out a list of the things you truly *don't* want to do, or don't like doing. Then, on the list, check off anything you're not really going to do anyway—and take it off the list. Get rid of it. Stop spending "anxiety energy" worrying about not doing something, and making yourself feel like you're not a quality person. Take that same energy and redirect it into something else.

List the Benefits—So You Can See the Results

In your career, or in building a business, there are things that have to be done to get the job done, of course.

So after you've fine-tuned your list of things you procrastinate on and gotten rid of the things you've decided you're *not* going to do, list the benefits of doing each item that remains on the list—so you can see the positive *results* of taking action. When you read the benefits, and see the value of taking action on the items on your list, you may want to recommit.

If it's something that has to be done, but you're really not going to do it anyway, give yourself permission to delegate. Try finding someone else to help you, or even to do it for you. And move on.

5. We don't take action if . . .
We have fear, or if we have to do something we're not used to doing.

The greatest enemy of success is fear.

I often wonder how many things we could do in our lives if we were not afraid to do them. *Imagine* what we could do in a month, or a year, if we were entirely without fear or self-doubt! We could do anything that's humanly possible to do.

But because of fear or uncertainty, often unconsciously, we put off doing things we're not used to doing. That's natural. It comes from an in-born psychological protection program that's designed to keep us from venturing too far from the nest, and maybe getting hurt.

But that same program that's designed to protect us also keeps us tethered to the tree—the safe place where we're secure and can't get hurt. As a child, attending your first day at school, you might have experienced the tug of that tether. (Or the first time you drove a car by yourself in traffic.)

Now, as adults, with holdovers from those "protection programs" from our past, we do most easily what seems *safest* for us—things we're comfortable doing. We may feel the excitement of the new challenge and the new rewards in front of us. But we also feel the doubts and the misgivings—just like we might have felt on our first day at school.

Doing Something You're Not Used to Doing

If I were to call you on the phone and invite you to go on stage with me in front of a few hundred or maybe a few thousand people, and give a 20-minute talk, would you look forward to speaking on stage, or would you avoid it if you could?

Think about something in your own life that you avoid because it's something you're not comfortable doing. It could be speaking in front of even a small group, or presenting your products to a stranger.

When you're faced with doing something that makes you uncomfortable, even if it's something you need to do, what do you often do instead, if procrastination is an issue for you? You either avoid it completely—or *put it off* as long as you can, and tell yourself, *"I'll do that later."* Some other time.

The result is, you put the action you were supposed to take *now* at the *bottom* of your list of things you have to do to reach the goal. So your fears push your goals further out of reach, unless you do something about it.

When You Lose Your Fear—You Gain Your Life

The solution to putting yourself into action when you have to do something that you're unsure of doing is *courage* and *practice*—until it's no longer new, or you're no longer afraid of doing it.

If you have to make a presentation in front of a group of people and tell them about your business and the way it's changing people's lives, make the presentation—as often as you can.

If, tomorrow, you have to make some phone calls you might otherwise have put off making, go ahead. Make the calls. (It's been my experience that no one has ever gotten shot over the telephone!)

If you have to counsel someone who needs your encouragement and your belief, but you're uncomfortable doing this, just talk from your heart. No matter what it is you have to do to move forward in your business or your life, take the plunge, have courage, and do it. And then do it again the next time.

In time, you'll look back and wonder why you ever worried about doing any of those things in the first place.

Now let's look at something you can do, beginning now, that will help.

163

Some Special Self-Talk for
Putting Yourself Into Action Now

Here is some Self-Talk that can help you put yourself into action. It is designed to help you see yourself as you were meant to be—alive, aware, in tune, on top, in touch, and *going for it!*

I put success into action by putting myself into action.

Because I choose to be successful, I choose to take action now—right now, today.

I get things done, on time and in the right way.

I do everything I need to do, when I need to do it.

I never wait for someone else to put me into motion. I enjoy motivating myself, and I'm good at putting myself into action.

I read my goal plan daily. I have a clear picture of my goals in my mind at all times.

I know that taking action on my plan is the secret to my success—and I take action every day.

I know that getting things done is nothing more than taking one step at a time. So I take the next step, and I keep moving.

I refuse to let obstacles stand in my way. I solve the problem and I move past it.

I never give up, and I never give in. I choose to keep moving, and I choose to win. I don't stop!

I get things done because I am in control of my goals, my time, and every action I take.

Right now, at this moment, I make the choice to succeed. Right now, I make the choice to take action.

I choose to reach my goals and I choose to win!

I choose to take action now!

When You Can't Seem to Get Anywhere, and Don't Know What to Do Next

When you can't seem to get moving, or you get stuck and stay there, it's usually the person in the mirror that's doing it. It's not the business, it's not the products, and it's not the goals you have. It may be just you, holding yourself back, or fighting your own progress. When that happens, take a break. Look at what you're doing from a fresh point of view. Ask yourself the question, *"What do I really want?"* Your answer will tell you what you should do next.

The most important thing you can do is to take yourself and your business seriously. (If you're presently an Arbonne consultant, at any level, take it seriously. What you're doing is not only a way to help others get better, but it's also a way of life that can change your entire future.)

So you should make every day count. That means taking every action step you can take to make it work for you. If you want to achieve the best from yourself, you have to put your *life* into action. That's not about what you're going to do next week. That's about what you're going to do right now, today and tomorrow.

When you start using each of the tools we've discussed up to now, you should begin to find yourself more focused, on track, moving forward and having a great time doing it. But what happens if, for a time, things just don't go your way? Will you stop, or will you stay with it?

The next gift will make sure you keep moving, and keep reaching your goals. It is the powerful gift of *never giving up*.

Chapter 13

The Gift of Never Giving Up

S ome people survive in spite of anything. They have that almost magical quality of being able to endure any adversity and somehow come out on top. They keep going no matter what. And they never give up.

The people who do that—those people who always overcome the obstacles, and excel in spite of them—are no different than you. They're not uniquely gifted. They've just learned how to keep moving *forward*, when other people *stop*.

You can do that too. You can keep moving forward. No matter what it is you're up against, there are some steps you can take to remain in control, keep your dreams in sight, keep moving forward, and reach your goal.

I'll tell you what those steps are, and how to apply them in your life right now, or any time you need to use them.

167

We're Always Told to Never Give Up— But Sometimes It Takes More Than That

In their life-changing books, self-help authors have told us that the ultimate choice each of us has is to set the goal, and never give up. They're right, of course, but "not giving up" is not always that simple, and it's not always easy to do.

My own conclusion is that the single idea of "never giving up" is one of the most important ideas for the fostering of personal success and personal growth—but we have to know *how* to do it. We have to know what steps to take to know whether we should quit—or whether we should seize the goal and never give up.

When Things Don't Work, There Are Those Who Stop—And Those Who Don't

This is a gift that you should always be ready to use when times are tough, when you're getting tired, or when you can no longer see the promise that started you on the road in the first place.

When that happens—and it happens to all of us many times—you'll have the choice to either keep going, or stop where you are. When you feel down or defeated, at that moment, what you *do* next will determine what *happens* next. You'll either draw back and invite defeat, or you'll stay with it and win.

Our Willingness to *Stay With It*, Is Based on How Much We *Believe* in the Outcome

To find the solution, we first have to understand the problem:

When things are working, we believe in the success of the moment. When things are not working, we doubt the success of the future.

When we're on top and going for it, and things are going our way, we never consider giving up. We keep moving forward with joy and enthusiasm for what we're doing. When life is *working*, all we want to do is keep doing it.

But now and then, as we've all discovered, life throws us some surprises. From time to time life doesn't work as well as we'd like it to. And if that down-turn in our once-happy forward progress lasts too long, we eventually run out of energy, and the dream that got us started starts to fade.

The problem is that we run out of "belief," or we run out of "dream." When that happens, it's like trying to keep driving the car when the car we're driving has run out of gas. We give in, and we give up on the goal, because we've lost our spirit for going on.

Five Steps to Never Giving Up

When you feel like you want to quit or give up, what should you do? What can you do? When that happens, here are five decisive steps that you can take, immediately. Each of the steps begins with a question, to be answered by you. Each of the questions is followed by a simple action step that you can take at any time you'd like to know whether to stop now, or stay with your goal:

1. Do you really want to quit, or do you still want to reach the goal?

Why did you want to reach this goal in the first place? Is it still a worthwhile goal, something you'd really like to achieve? Is your goal or your dream more important than the problems that have gotten in your way? Is your goal big enough or worthy enough for you to do everything you can do to reach the goal?

Action Step #1: *Decide whether or not the goal is still important to you.*

2. Are you willing to invest the time and the energy it will take to make this goal happen?

If this is something you wanted to do, and you've decided you still want to do it, are you willing to *invest* whatever it takes to do it?

This could be a serious commitment of your time and your energies. If you can't give an unqualified "yes" to the desire to do it, you have to go back and rethink the value of the goal and whether you really want to do it or not. If your answer to this question is a resounding *"Yes,"* you have a good chance of reaching the goal.

Action Step #2: *Make a new agreement that you're willing to make an investment in your goal—to bring it to life and make it happen.*

3. Are you willing to recognize that "obstacles" are nothing more than the natural check points you have to pass to reach your goal?

Somewhere along the road to building our independence, or our future, we all have to accept the fact that problems and obstacles are just part of the game—part of life. (If we don't encounter obstacles, we haven't left home.) They're normal and natural check points that let us know we're on the journey.

The best solution is to make the decision to agree to deal with them, be glad you're on the journey, and focus your mind on the end result. Instead of letting any of the normal "problems" of life get you down, practice looking at them as something that *everyone* has to deal with—and so do you. So you can accept them, agree to deal with them, and move on.

Action Step #3: *Decide to see obstacles as normal, and very natural, steps to success.*

4. If you really want to reach the goal, are you willing to "believe," once again, that you can do it?

Wanting to do something is one thing. Being willing to *believe* in yourself long enough to do it is another.

Since believing in yourself, about anything, is a choice, this is one you'll have to decide to do. You have to choose to believe. If you do that, and make the *choice* to believe in what you want to achieve, you have, in that moment, increased immeasurably your chances of reaching your goal.

Action Step #4: *Make the choice to **believe** in yourself—and **believe** you can do it.*

5. Are you willing to restate the goal, now, and restate your absolute *determination* to reach it?

The achievement of all good goals and dreams ultimately gets down to personal *determination.* Your best achievements in life will always be the result of your own personal "will" to make them happen. Whatever you dedicate yourself to most is what you will create most. If you want something important, you have to make the commitment to creating it—and have the fortitude to stay with it.

You will always get what you want in your life in direct proportion to your determination to have it.

Action Step #5: *Restate your personal determination to reach the goal.*

"Giving up" shouldn't be a passive event that happens as a result of letting something worthwhile go by the wayside, without your personal thought or direction. If you want to let go of a goal or a project or even a dream, you should do so with intent, *consciously* making the decision.

So the next time you feel like "giving up," no matter what it is, take a few moments and read through those questions and those five steps, once again.

Then, whether you decide to stop or quit, or to go on and reach the goal, you will have made a conscious choice in the matter of what to do next. And you won't leave either "giving up" or "staying with it" up to chance. You will have made a choice. And the choice will be yours.

If You Believe in the Goal, Never Give Up

If it was up to the opinion of a journalism teacher I had in high school, I might never have written my first book. And from that experience, I learned a great lesson about never giving up.

I started out with an attempt at writing a book when I was about 14 years old. At the time, I was just a kid who had a goal to write a book that would help people change their lives for the better. But after writing the first three chapters of that book, I came to the realization that as a 14-year-old, I had no idea what I was talking about. I didn't know enough, yet, to write the book.

I tried writing that book again when I was 17 and a junior in high school. By that time I had read and been impressed by life-changing books by authors like Norman Vincent Peale and Napoleon Hill, and I had begun to formulate some early personal growth ideas for myself.

I took the manuscript of my book to my journalism class

in high school, and asked my teacher to read it and tell me what she thought. I had worked hard on it, and by now my goal was even stronger to write a book that would help people get better, and that would be published all over the world—a lofty goal for someone who was only 17 years old.

I had given the teacher my manuscript after class on Friday and asked her if she would look at it over the weekend. After a long wait, Monday finally came, and I couldn't wait to get to journalism class and hear my teacher tell me I had written a sure-to-be best-seller. At the end of her class period, she asked me to stay behind, and after the other students had all left, my teacher sat on the corner of her desk and waved my manuscript in front of me as she bestowed her judgement on me and my book.

"You will *never* write a best-selling book!" she said. And then she went on to tell me that I didn't have the skill, the words, or the endurance to stay with it, write a book, and see it published. "Besides all that," she added, "almost *no one* writes a book that becomes a best-seller. You wouldn't have a chance!" Her condemnation was a stunning blow to my young self-concept and to my lifetime goal.

It would be years more before I would finally see my goal come to life, but although I had suffered a setback that nearly stopped me from writing ever again, I had decided not to give up.

I met that teacher again several years later at a high school class reunion. She was sitting in a chair surrounded by three or four decades of past students. When I approached her and said hello, I didn't mention what she had told me years earlier about my manuscript and goal. I doubt she would have remembered. But I did give her a *gift*. It was a stack of six different hardcover books I had written—each on the subject of personal growth—that were being published in sixty-four countries around the world.

(Although I didn't remind my old teacher that she had told me I would never write a best-selling book, considering what my books were about—personal growth and believing in yourself—I did suggest that she might want to *read* one or two of them.)

The most important lesson I learned from my teacher's early denial of my potential and then, ultimately, my own choice to do it anyway, no matter how long it took, was that endurance wins. There is no power on earth that is stronger than determination.

A Picture of Determination the Whole World Watched

A number of years ago, a small girl fell into a well. You may remember the story. Baby Jessica, at just 18 months old, fell into an abandoned well shaft in Midland, Texas. For the next life-threatening days of little Jessica's life, rescuers worked feverishly to bring her back to the surface and retrieve her from the well. Every hour they worked, they never considered what it would take to bring her out. Their only thought and prayer was that they would find little Jessica, and that when they did, she would be alive and breathing, and she would be safe.

The crews who were trying to save Jessica struggled for 58 hours to get her out of the 8-inch-wide pipe her little body was trapped in. While all that went on, the whole world watched and waited.

None of the rescuers on the scene thought for a moment about ever giving up. And none of them did. In so doing, they saved the life of a little 18-month-old child.

Because they refused to give up, 17 years later, in May, 2004, in a small town near Midland, Texas, Jessica graduated from high school.

The determination you and I need to make our own lives work may not seem as dramatic as the kind of determination that saved little Jessica and gave her a chance at life. But it is that same sense of being unwilling to give up or give in—expressed in the stories of the lives we live now, every day—that gives *us* a chance at making something of our *own* lives.

If You Use this Gift, You *Will* Reach Your Goals

Whatever it is, if you refuse to quit or give up, if it's reachable at all—you *will* reach the goal. If you use the gift of *never giving up*, every day, there's no telling what you can do.

If you really want to, you *can* travel the world. You *can* help other people get better. You *can*, if you want to, be free from your day job and work for yourself. You *can* drive a new white Mercedes. You *can* create financial freedom for you and the people you love. If you're an Arbonne consultant, you *can* reach the highest level in the business you choose to reach. If it can be done at all, you *can* do anything you imagine you can do. *Think* it, *see* it clearly, set a goal to *do* it, and *never give up.*

If you do that, and refuse to give up on your dream, you could soon be lying on a beach in somewhere like St. Thomas or Cancun, re-reading this book and thinking, "All the people who told me to never give up were right. *All I had to do was never give up.*"

And that would be true. When you want to create exceptional personal growth in your life in every way, and when you want to achieve your greatest goals, if you want to *win*—use the gifts.

And while you're using them, *never give up.*

The next gift will make it easy to put *all* of these tools of growth into practice. In fact, this next gift makes *everything* better. It is the wonderful gift of doing something you *love*.

Chapter 14

The Gift of Doing Something You Love

S ome people are completely happy in the job they're in, and they wouldn't change it for anything.

For those people who *are* completely happy in their work, I always encourage them. They have a job; they work to earn a living, and in the process, they create a life that works for them.

But there is the other, much larger group of people who go to work every day, when they really wish they didn't *have* to. Either their job isn't rewarding enough personally, or it doesn't bring in enough income, or perhaps it's a job with no real future, or it may just be the wrong job in the first place. Whatever the case, for them, going to work every day just isn't as fulfilling as it ought to be.

The problem is that all too many people put up with their job or career, even if it's the wrong one, because they really don't know anything better to do. And yet, as much of our life as we spend on the job, we ought to be doing something that *builds* our life instead of just using it up. We only have so many hours in a day. (We only have so many hours in a *life!*) We ought to be spending that time doing something that is uplifting and fulfilling—and certainly never just "putting in time."

So how do you become one of the group of people who love the work they do so completely that they see it as a career made in heaven?

How You See the Work You Do Now

Let's say there's a list of people—and the work they do—and everyone's name is on the list. Yours is there too.

At the very top of the list are the names of people who love their work so completely that they wouldn't trade it for anything else. These people have a great job, enviable job satisfaction, plenty of reward and fulfillment, a chance to earn any income they want, and a never-ending opportunity to keep growing. So the people at the top of this list are in the "Completely Fulfilled" section of the list.

The Other End of the List

On the far extreme—on the very bottom part of the list—are the people who see their jobs in the exact opposite way. This is the "Completely Unfulfilled" section of the list.

These are the people who work at the job they have for one reason only—because they have to. They have to earn enough money to pay their basic bills—and they usually have trouble doing even that. They hate going to work on Mondays (or any other day, for that matter), they don't like the work they do, and they often have problems with the people they work with —because *those* people are just as unhappy as *they* are.

These people have no future in the job they're in, but they're too far down to know what anything better looks like. So they stay where they are, and eventually convince themselves "that's just the way life is," and that there's nothing they can do about it.

The People In the Middle

In the middle—between the "Completely Fulfilled" people at the top of the list and the "Completely Unfulfilled" people at the bottom of the list—is everyone else.

This middle group is the largest group by far. In this middle part of the list, we find some people who are reasonably happy, and many others who are happy now and then but most of the time wish they could be doing something different or better.

When you ask some people in this broad, middle group how things are going, they'll often say things like "A job is a

180

job," or "Another day, another dollar." They're earning an income and they're getting by; they're doing "okay."

There are also people in this middle section of the list who have quite a lot to show for their efforts—a good home, a nice car or two, and most of the symbols of reasonable success. And if not *blissful* with their career choices, they're not completely *unhappy*, either. They may like the social aspects of work, and they have the chance to get promotions and pay increases, at least up to a point.

Living for Job Security

Many of those people won't ever own the company, but they'll do *all right*. They'll still have to show up on time, of course; they'll still have to limit their lunch hour or the amount of time they take off to someone else's demands, and they'll never be their own boss—but they accept all that. That's part of the "sacrifice," they tell themselves, for having job security.

But while they're sacrificing much of their lives for job security, many of these "reasonably successful" people often feel a nagging sense of dissatisfaction deep within them, a lack of hope to ever do much better, and ultimately, a diminishing belief in themselves.

They hear a voice inside themselves that tells them they were meant to do so much *more*—that there is a greater value to life than just *"doing all right."* It's a quiet, constant nudge from their promised self, asking them to remember who they were really meant to be in the first place.

Of those who hear that voice, some of them will continue,

181

as they have for years, to push it into the background noise of their lives, bothered by its message of, *"What are you doing with your life?"*—but seemingly unwilling or unable to take action to do anything about it.

Others who hear that voice *listen* to it—and eventually follow its guidance and do something about it. When they do, they begin to live a life that lifts them *up*, recognizes their *potential*, finds their *promise*, and brings it to life.

Where Are You on the List?

In your own life right now, when it comes to your work or career, if you had to find your name on that list, where would you look? The bottom, the middle, or the top? Wherever you find yourself on the list, talk to the voice within you. Ask yourself if where you are now, or where you're clearly going, *is exactly what you want.* If the voice inside you tells you that your potential is greater than the direction you're following, then that's a message worth listening to. *That's* a message that could change your life.

Is What You're Doing Now What You Really *Want* to Do?

In a 24-hour day, at least during the work week, we sleep for about 8 hours, work for another 8 hours or so, and have a few more hours before and after we go to work. In the world we live in today, the hours we have are spent sleeping, getting up, getting ready, going to work, working, going home, being tired, watching television, and going to bed. And then, the next day, we do it all over again.

There are a lot of people who do that, and there's certainly nothing wrong with doing that—*if that's exactly what you want to do.*

The problem is that if you gave most of the people who do that every day the chance to suddenly stop doing it *forever*—like by giving them a winning lottery ticket—they would never do it again. The only reason they're following a tedious daily cycle like that is because they feel they *have* to—as though they have no other choice.

Which means that if they could find a better way, most of them would *not* get up, go to work, come home, watch television and go to bed—and then do it again the next day, and the next. If they believed they had a choice to do it differently, they would.

If You Won the Lottery *Today*, What Would You Want to Do *Tomorrow*?

Lottery winners never stay in unfulfilling jobs for years after they win a million or so dollars, or even a small win of a few hundred thousand dollars. (Most of them quit their jobs in a few days.) Why is that? It's because they suddenly discovered that, with the newfound freedom of their new income, the "job" they had previously dedicated so much of their life to was not really that "rewarding" in the first place.

Which brings us to an important question: "What would *you* want to do tomorrow, if you won the lottery today?"

If, tomorrow morning, you suddenly had more than enough

money in the bank to live for the next years and beyond, enough for a great home and a great lifestyle, would you go back to the same job you have right now? And would you want to *stay* there for the next five years, or even longer?

If you would stay where you are now work-wise, then you're probably doing something you genuinely love doing, and you have a good reason to stay. It's not just about the money you're earning—it's about the fulfillment you're finding.

However, if after winning the lottery today, you would change your job tomorrow, or as soon as you could appropriately do so, that tells you something else. If that's the case, your job is not only not the purpose in your life, but also *not* how you want to spend your life. If you didn't have to keep your job, you wouldn't.

The meaning of all this is, if you could do anything you really wanted to do, it *may* not be what you're doing now. For most of us, if we could do anything we wanted to, it would probably not be called a "job." It would be something much better than that.

(Have you answered the question for yourself? *If you won the lottery today, what would you want to do tomorrow?*)

Finding a Career Path That Lets You Win "Life's Lottery"

Imagine having a career path—not just a job, but something you did that was so fulfilling and enriching that you couldn't wait to get up in the morning. It would be as though instead of winning the lottery (which the odds tell you is not likely to happen), the right *career path* would give you the *same rewards*—and more!

What an uplifting choice that would be, to only do something for a living that you really loved to do! The kind of job or career where people say, "I can't believe I get paid for this." Or, "I love my work. I can't imagine doing anything else."

Unfortunately, we hear people say things like that now and then. But *only* now and then. It wasn't until I began to interview Arbonne consultants that I heard so *many* people say the same kind of thing again and again. And that got my attention. When hundreds of thousands of people around us go to work every day wishing they were doing something *else*—and then, when virtually everyone I was interviewing for research on a book told me they *love* what they do and wouldn't trade it for anything, I took notice.

When people find a career path doing something they love to do, they begin to feel good about themselves in whole new ways. Their self-esteem goes up, they appreciate every day in a better way, and they actually find the joy, the freedom, and the fulfillment of truly *living* their life.

And when that career path also gives them a whole new lease on life financially, along with the freedom to live their lives on their own schedule, the thought of ever going back to that old job routine of getting up in the morning to go to work for someone else is no longer an option.

The Importance of Finding Financial Freedom

I've known people who have been fortunate enough to

have found the "perfect path" in the work they do in their lives. But, without exception, of all of the people I've known, not one of them would tell you that she or he found that perfect path by having what we would call just a "job."

If you really want to have control of your time and your life, you have to have *freedom* in your life—and that means you have to have a certain amount of *financial* freedom as well. Most of the people you'll ever meet, no matter where you meet them, even if it's on a sailboat in the Caribbean, will have to be back at work on Monday.

When I began interviewing Arbonne consultants, I met a surprising number of people who didn't have to be back at "work" on Monday. They work, of course. And they take their work seriously. But those who have decided to build their own businesses—and along with that, their own lives —are finding not only the work they love, but also the financial rewards to create freedom in the *rest* of their lives as well.

What Will You Do With the Most Important Time of Your Life?

I mentioned earlier that we sleep about 8 hours a day, work for another 8 hours, and have 8 remaining hours—when we're usually tired—to take care of the necessities of the day and get everything done that needs to be done. (And then, with that schedule, we wonder why we aren't able to find enrichment and fulfillment in our lives.)

The important message of that observation is this: in sixty years of adult life, from the age of 20 on, if you sleep eight hours a night, you will be *asleep* for *20* out of those 60 years.

You'll also have another six or eight hours each day to take care of the *necessities of life* around you, and have time off for yourself when you can find it—so that means you'll spend another 20 years doing that.

But, the important question is, "what will you do with the *rest* of the time—the *most important, active, hours you have each day*—the best years of your life?" You'll either give *that* huge part of your life *away*—working at a job, *for someone else*—or you'll change your mind, and seize your time for yourself!

For most of us, giving a third of our life away to a job, working for someone else, would not be called "freedom."

Freedom is doing what you want to do, when you want to do it.

People who are limited by the choices they make in their career paths often feel they can do nothing more than go to work each day, and accept their pay. They find it hard to believe that it doesn't have to be that way. Yet, those same individuals, somewhere inside themselves, know the truth about giving their lives away to a job. If they were given a good chance to break out of the circumstances they find themselves in, most of them would jump at the chance.

It is when you love what you do that you love your life most. That's when you're the most fulfilled. That's when you *live*—and feel more alive each day. That's when your spirit *soars*.

You Get to Choose the Life
That's Best for You

When it comes to what you choose to do for a living, there are two things that count most. They are: *things that bring you income*, and *things that fulfill your life*. Most people find one or the other. They either live their lives for the income they produce, or they live their lives for the personal fulfillment they seek. Or they work for a semblance of both.

After three decades of studying successful people, it's been my experience that you *can* have the best of both worlds. You can have financial freedom, and you can have personal enrichment and fulfillment. But it doesn't happen by accident or by just hoping for it. You have to *choose* it. The people who have "freedom" and successful lives, somewhere along the way, made the *choice* to have them.

The truth is, no matter where you are in your life right now, you get to set the goal and you get to set the rules. *You* get to decide whether or not you do something you would most love to do—or put it off, wait for some other time, or never do it at all.

Your "deal" with life could be something like this:

"I choose to do with my life, whatever it sends my way, live with it, put up with it, and accept it in the best way that I can."

Or you can make a decidedly *different* deal with the rest of your life:

"With the life I have in front of me, I choose to do some-

thing I love to do, every day, and something that will fulfill me in every way."

Many people will never take the time to make that choice—or to rethink the career choices that put them where they are now. They're too busy living in the cycle of going to work and coming home to ever stop long enough to recognize that they still have a choice.

What Will You Choose to Do?

Will you give yourself the gift of doing something you love? Or will you give in to the demands of everyday living, set your own dreams aside, and wait for another time?

If you want to do something you would love to do, then I encourage you to *do* what you want to do! As you do that, you'll eventually get past the worry of making the change. Life will go on in spite of the uncertainty or the fear. Make the choice to do what you would like to do most, outline your plan, and take the first step.

When you do the things you love to do most, you fulfill more of your own personal purpose in life, and bring to that purpose the essence of who you are. And when you give *that* kind of spirit and life to your dreams, you find the value and the *joy* of living. That's something worth finding!

When the Work You Do Was Made for You

The difference between working at something you love and at something you don't, affects virtually everything about you. It doesn't just affect your income or your professional progress; it affects *everything*.

When your work is in *harmony* with who you are inside, your whole world changes. Suddenly you find that your work *gives* you energy—instead of stealing your energy from you. You can still get tired, but it's a *worthwhile* kind of tired. You find your days are more uplifting; instead of feeling like too many days are overcast and gray, you see the sunlight. Now you feel you're doing something of value, something you were meant to do. Now, instead of not wanting to talk about your work, you want to *share* it with everyone!

When the relationship you have with your work is healthy and energizing, it will show in everything you do and everything you touch. Your family will feel it, your friends will know it, and your mood and your day will show it.

Instead of feeling lost or out of step, when you love the work you do, life is good; you're in touch with who you are and what you're doing. And you can't *wait* to get back to "work" on Monday.

When You Want to Do Something You Love— But Others Don't Want You to Change

Sometimes people around us, especially those who depend on us most, don't want us to make any changes. But if you have a good plan, moving forward and making positive changes can be one of the healthiest things you can do, both for yourself and for the people who rely on you.

We either live in the shadows of our "could be" potential, or we take the step and do it. If we had believed in ourselves *enough*, we'd have known that *going for it* is what we wanted to do in the first place.

When you start talking to your friends, and especially your family, about doing something new (even if, for the present, you're keeping your day job), some of them may hope you'll soon come back to your senses, be happy with the life you've got, and get back to normal. But "normal" doesn't necessarily mean "good"—or *right*. Normal just means that's the way people have done it in the past—even if "normal" wasn't very fulfilling and wasn't even the career path they should have followed in the first place.

When you choose to grow in your own life, and you hear that voice within you reminding you of the promise of your own future—when that voice gets loud enough, then it's time to take the step. When you do that, trust that the people who love you the most will have faith in your judgement, and help you move forward and reach the goal.

People who fear moving forward, those who *fail* to take the steps in their lives that could count the most, never live up to their greatest potential. They just forget the dreams they had of what could have been, and live a life of something less.

Something That's *Essential* for You— And a *Blessing* for Them

If you want to have fulfillment in your life, doing some-

191

thing you love is not selfish or self-centered; it's *essential*. The myth (that many of us were programmed to believe) is that everyone and everything else—family, job, and other "responsibilities"—come first, and that *we* come second. That way of thinking is the opposite of how successful living really works.

If you do something you love to do, something that is so enriching that your life is in harmony and balance because of it, you will do *more* for your family, *more* for your income, and *more* for the world around you than you could ever do by putting yourself last or following the wrong path to your future.

Find something you *love* to do, and do it. When you do that, you and everyone around you will benefit. And instead of just finding a *job* that works, you'll find a *life* that works.

Now let's look at one more gift. It is about you; it is an exciting gift, and it's the greatest gift of all.

Chapter 15

The Greatest Gift of All

T he greatest gift of all is, of course, your *"Self."* The greatest gift is *you*.

The final gift, then, and the greatest earthly gift you can ever receive, is the gift of *you—and making your own dreams come true.* It is the gift of who you are and what you can do with the rest of your life today, and every incredible day you have in front of you.

It may be an unusual thing to imagine that what happens next in your life could actually be up to you. But, if you think about it, it *is* up to you. The *real* direction of your life will be determined by what you decide to do next.

You might think that your job, your family, your relationships, your responsibilities, or the demands of the rest of the world around you will determine what you do next in your life. The truth is, what you want from here on out in your own life not only *counts*—but your whole future is up to what you *dream*, and what you do next.

The Dreams You Dream When You're "Asleep"—and the Dreams You Dream When You're "Wide Awake"

Most people, when they sleep, dream. But some people have learned to dream during the day, when they're wide awake—and then go on to give *life* to their dreams. Few of your "sleeping" dreams really come true. But when you're "wide awake" and dreaming, you have the chance to make your dreams come to life.

I'd like to share with you a parable about making dreams come true. It's the story of "Sechi and the Angel." This is a story that could be about you, or anyone you know.

The Story of Sechi and the Angel

There was a woman named Sechi who, night after night, dreamed of being a princess, or royal in some way, or being someone *special*. In her dream, while she slept, Sechi was fulfilled in every part of her life. She was respected, listened

194

to, successful in every way, and had everything she needed to live her life in every positive way. It was a wonderful dream, and she dreamed it often.

But during the day, Sechi's life was very different. During the day, Sechi felt she was no more than "average." She believed she was someone who was not special or important in any way.

So each day, instead of living the life of her dreams, Sechi lived her days in an ordinary way. She worked to raise her family, worked at her job, and did everything she could to make life work.

But as Sechi worked to make her life work in the right way each day, night after night, she dreamed the same dream. Each night, while she slept, Sechi dreamed that she was *different*. She was *better* than who she was in her everyday life during the day. Each night, in her dream, she held a magical wand in her hand. And with a wave of that wand, she could create anything she could imagine.

In her night-time dream, she could *fly!* In *that* dream she could do *anything!* She could wish for something to happen in a certain way, and it would happen—in just that way! Freedom, goals, dreams, and wishes were hers—anything at all was hers for the asking—just by wanting it, and by the waving of her magical wand.

But once again, each morning, upon awakening, the wand and the dream would always fade away. During the *real* day, Sechi believed she would *never* be someone special.

During the years that Sechi dreamed her wonderful dream at night and lived her ordinary life during the day, though she did her best to live a good life, she felt unfulfilled. "There is no magic," she thought. Her *real* life, the one she lived when

195

she was awake, was the only life she would ever have. And that life, the one without the magic, would have to do.

But then, one important night, something changed. Sechi had a *different* dream. In this dream she had a very special visitor. At first she thought that the shining image she saw might have been a departed loved one, someone who was protecting her in some way, or watching over her.

Sechi finally decided that the visitor in her dream that night was an angel, a special visitor who had come to show her what to do next. But whoever it was in that dream on that one important night, spoke to Sechi while she slept.

"You have a gift," the angel said. *"You have many gifts. But there is one special gift, above all others, that will give you everything you have only been dreaming of.*

And then the shining spirit said, *"You have everything within you that you have ever dreamed to be. You just haven't used your gifts and lived your real dreams for your-self."*

And then the angelic spirit did an unusual thing. *"Give me your wand,"* her vision said. *"The magic wand you use in your dreams each night. You don't need it anymore."* And with that, the bright, shining angel gently took the wand from Sechi's hand and said,

"Instead of the wand, use your mind.
Instead of just wishing, use your heart.
Instead of only dreaming, use the moments *you have in front of you."*

And then the angel said, *"It's time to make your life work, in every wonderful way. To help you reach your real dreams, I'm going to give you now, some very special gifts."*

And then the angel tapped Sechi's wand twelve times— once for each of the gifts she would give to Sechi. *"I've waited a long time to give these gifts to you, but you are ready now. It is time for your real life to begin."* And then, gently touching the wand to Sechi's forehead with each gift, Sechi's angel gave her the twelve gifts:

"The first gift I'm giving to you is the gift of always having others around you who believe in you, and who will teach you how to become the best of yourself.

The second gift is the gift of "choice." This gift will help you make the smallest and the greatest of choices, which, if you choose well, will make your life work as wonderfully as your dreams.

The third gift is to always live your life in a way that will help other people grow and become better. By helping others, your life will grow in a greater way than you have ever known.

The fourth gift by itself, will help you do more than anything you might ever have dreamed. It is the gift of always believing in yourself.

The fifth gift I give to you is the gift of releasing the past and opening your mind to the real you, the one that is about to become.

The sixth gift will help you see your life, and everything in it, in the best possible way, so you see the good each day.

The seventh gift I bestow upon you is the gift of finding what is truly important to you in the life you have in front of you, so you'll always know what to seek most.

The eighth gift is the gift of always knowing the path to follow, and choosing what you will do next about each of the dreams you want to come true.

The ninth gift will help you own your time each day, and will give you the freedom to use all of the other gifts you are being given.

The tenth gift will help you do what you need to do now, each day, instead of waiting for some other time to make your life the precious and important life that it was meant to be.

The eleventh gift is the gift of strength and endurance, so that your spirit will go on, even when the world around you would tell you to give up and put your dreams to rest.

The twelfth gift is given to you to remind you that it is only when you do something you truly love, that you will truly love the life you are living."

"Those are your gifts," the angel said. *"But to own them and to make them yours, you must use them. Use each of the gifts you have been given, and you will receive the greatest gift of all. And that will be the gift of your Self."*

Then the angel smiled at Sechi, with the most loving countenance she had ever seen. *"If you use those gifts, then you won't need the wand you have used in your dreams while you slept. You won't need hopes, or wishes, or wants, or night-time dreams. If you use the gifts I have given you, each day, you will receive the one gift that is above all others. And you will live the life you have only dreamed of living."*

And then, as the dream began to fade, the angel gave Sechi one final message. They were the words that Sechi would remember always, and the words that would change her life forever:

"Use the gifts, and you will live your dreams."

If you do that—if you use the gifts, and if you make the choice to live your dreams, no matter what they are, you will live the life you've always wanted to live.

The angel's final message to Sechi is the best and most lasting message I could give to you.

"Use the gifts, and you will live your dreams."

When you live your dreams, you can do *anything*.

Information and Resources You Can Use:

Self-Talk CDs
To order professionally recorded Self-Talk CDs:
www.SelfTalkStore.com

"The Gift"
To order the book *"The Gift"*:
www.OrderTheGift.com

"Teaching The Gift"
12-Session Instructional Program
with Leader's Guide and Student Workbooks:
www.OrderTheGift.com

Goal-Setting Programs
Online goal-setting program - *www.goals-on-line.com*
Goal-setting for Kids - *www.Goals4Kids.com*

About Arbonne International
To learn more about Arbonne products or becoming
an Independent Arbonne Consultant, contact the
Arbonne representative who introduced you to the
Arbonne products or business program.
For more information - www.arbonne.com.

To contact Dr. Helmstetter:
shad@shadhelmstetter.com